MW00967226

WE CAN HEAR YOU JUST FINE

WE CAN HEAR YOU JUST FINE

Clarifications from the Kentucky School for the Blind

Matthew Caudill

Haley Hall

Shane Lowe

Madelyn Loyd

Selena Tirey

Kianna Waller

Cherish Willis

Edited by Joe Manning

LOUISVILLE
STORY
PROGRAM

Louisville Story Program
851 South 4th Street
Louisville, KY 40203

www.louisvillestoryprogram.org
502.583.3326

This book is made possible by generous support from the Kentucky Arts Council, Brown-Forman, the Snowy Owl Foundation, the Arthur K. Smith Family Foundation, the Kentucky School for the Blind Charitable Foundation, the Gilbert Foundation, and the Louisville Downtown Lions Club.

ISBN 978-0-9914765-2-7
Library of Congress Control Number: 2016950138

Book design by Shellee Marie Jones
Cover art by Letitia Quesenberry

Printed in Canada

Some names and identifying details have been changed to protect the privacy of individuals.

CONTENTS

INTRODUCTION

When the Kentucky School for the Blind was chartered in 1842, it was only the third state-supported educational institution for the blind and visually impaired in America. Since that time, students from all over the Commonwealth have come to KSB to learn how to better navigate a sighted, and frequently indifferent, world. They come in the belief that success and dignity cannot be "disabled" or "impaired," and the book you hold in your hands is a demonstration of this belief.

In the 2015-2016 school year, the Louisville Story Program partnered with the Kentucky School for the Blind to provide a college-level creative nonfiction workshop for seven student-authors with a desire to tell their stories. Their literary aims became a paid internship, and four days a week they read nonfiction by renowned authors, considered critical essays, and discussed elements of craft. They also wrote a great deal. Throughout the academic year, and into the summer, they accepted rigorous instruction and feedback on composition and revision. Writing on computers, cell phones, and braille writers, and editing their prose with their eyes, or with assistive technologies, they learned how to distill experience and emotion into compelling, relatable storytelling. This is the first anthology of its kind ever printed, and we believe that you will find it compeling and relatable in the utmost.

By digging deep to tell their stories, and by inviting members of their home communities to describe their own experiences in thoughtful oral history interviews, these authors have written chapters that investigate the ways we remember our lives, and the degree to which we are willing to recognize ourselves in our neighbors.

In our workshops, when we discussed what this book was intended to do, we frequently used the metaphor of sound as a means of determining location. The image is of one voice in a very large room bouncing off of the walls, floors, and ceiling. Then another voice is added, and the echoes create a more accurate understanding of this shared space. We discussed the benefit of many voices used in this way: calling out, reverberating, reflecting, responding, and defining the contours of a room, or of a community.

Rich with lived experience, irreverence, trial, hope, humor, and triumph, the narratives in these pages imply a question, one that's tucked into the title. In these chapters, Madelyn, Selena, Haley, Matthew, Shane, Kianna, and Cherish invite you to listen. Can you hear them?

Joe Manning

Photo by Jessica Ebelhar

MADELYN
LOYD

CHANGING FOCUS

When I was a little girl, I couldn't see a thing out of my right eye because it wasn't in my head. It had been removed when I was eighteen months old because I had a form of ocular cancer called retinoblastoma. In its place, I have a prosthetic eye made of acrylic. As a little kid, I wasn't always very responsible with my fake eye; it was all a big game to me. Getting it dirty or losing it was an easy way to make my mother frantic and spazzy, which I found hilarious. I'd roll the eye across the floor in Walmart, or put the eye in my mouth, or use the eye to play hide-and-seek: I hide the eye, Mom goes to seek it. My favorite hiding spot was in the toilet. I had to learn that most little girls did not put fake eyes in their mouths, and that I needed to take care of it. I had to clean it every day so that I would look nice, especially during allergy season. Like most kids with allergies, I got a runny or stuffy nose, but I also got a runny, crusty fake eye that needed to be cleaned.

I get a new eye every four years or so because I'm still growing. It's actually a pretty cool and relaxing process, and the man who makes my eyes for me is truly remarkable. Glenn Reams is a highly regarded ocularist, and his prosthetic eyes are his art. He's also an extremely caring individual and a blast to talk to. Glenn's office looks just like an eye doctor's room, with a chair that raises and reclines. When I was a kid, I'd always sit up in the chair and demand that my mom hit the pedals to make it rise and fall as we waited for Glenn.

He comes in, takes out my current eye and examines it, prods around in my eye socket for a bit, and then the magic starts. The stuff that he pours into my often-swollen eye socket feels cool and glorious. He lets the goo sit for a while to firm up, and then sticks a toothpick in the center to remove it. Mom and I leave for a few hours while the eye is glazed and baked. When we come back, Glenn sticks the new eye in to make sure everything fits, then takes it out and starts on my favorite part. Looking at my real eye, he paints the fake one right in from of me. It's amazing to watch, and when he is finished my prosthetic looks totally realistic. The eye has to be glazed and baked again, then polished, and then I walk out with a new eyeball.

I've been told that my eyes are hazel, but my sister Brooklyn tells me that my left eye, the real one, turns blue when I'm angry, and green when I'm relaxed. My fake eye always stays hazel.

I have zero vision in my fake eye (obviously), and only about 40% vision in my left eye. I can't make out details and I have no depth perception. Steps blend together and look like part of the floor, so when I go down stairs, I do it by feel.

Visual impairment is all I've ever known. I have never been sad or ashamed of being blind; it's a part of me, just like my red hair and my freckles, and I know I am just as capable as anybody. Since I was a child, people have asked me if one day there was some technology that could make me see perfectly, is that something I would do? I always say no. I love myself, and I love the people I have come to meet through my blindness and the opportunities I've had as a result. My blindness doesn't define me: I define how it affects me, and I have never let it affect me in a negative way. Never will.

When most people see a person walking down the street with a white cane, they are probably amazed that a blind person is out walking on their own. Then again, most people are amazed that blind people can tie their own shoes.

Everyone is different,
but most blind people
won't take too kindly to
being randomly grabbed
and helped
across the street.

Photo by Jessica Ebelhar

There are many other misconceptions about those of us who have a visual impairment. First of all, we are blind, not deaf. There is a difference. We don't know sign language. We can hear you just fine. It's our eyes that aren't as good as yours. We rely on our hearing a lot more than the average Joe, but we do not have super hearing—we're just paying closer attention.

Another misconception about blind people is that we are completely and utterly helpless. We're not. We can do anything that sighted people can do, except drive a car legally—we work, we play games, we clean, we cook, we love. Everyone is different, but most blind people won't take too kindly to being randomly grabbed and helped across the street. Don't be offended if we decline your help; we have self-advocacy drilled into our heads from day one, and we try our best to be independent. If we need your help, we will tell you.

Also, not all blind people are totally blind. Different people have different amounts of vision. Some people, like myself, are totally blind in one eye, but have functional or usable vision in the other, while some people can only see shadows of figures or light, and others see nothing at all. Most people think it is rude to ask a blind person about their vision, but it isn't. Blindness is a part of our lives, it is something we are very comfortable with, and we don't mind talking about it.

I was always excited to take the five-hour road trip for my eye doctor appointment in Cincinnati. I used to see the doctor every day, then every week, then every month, and now I go once a year. I got to stop and eat yummy food, and I got to hang out with my funny eye doctor, Dr. Augsburger, whom I fondly called Dr. Hamburger. I never remember calling him anything else. To this day, when I go for my check up, my nana texts me and tells me to say hi to Dr. Hamburger for her.

One particular visit when I was five stands out in my memory. In the parking lot of Hamburger's office, I whined and complained as my mom ran a brush through my hair, straightened my clothes, and handed me a baby wipe to clean the eye boogers off of my prosthetic eye. She always thought I had to look perfect. I didn't really understand this because it was just Dr. Hamburger. As we made our way inside, I could tell Mom was nervous, as always. I never understood why she got antsy about a check-up; I didn't understand a lot back then.

I trotted into the familiar waiting room and called out happily to the receptionist/assistant. I loved Beth, she was the best, so kind and funny. She always gave me animal stickers at the end of my appointment. What better way to win a five-year-old's heart? After a few minutes of chatting with me, Beth took me back to test my vision and put in eye drops to dilate my eye. I didn't tell my mom about this until I was older, but I didn't want her being back there when I had to read the eye chart on the wall because I got embarrassed when I got to the letters I couldn't see. I knew that if I was like other kids, I'd be able to read it just fine. I also hated the eye drops, especially the numbing drops, which felt like hot needles being carelessly dropped into my eye. My mom pulled me onto her lap and hugged me tight as Beth put in the dreaded drops. After every drop, my mom would gently pat my eye with a tissue. "Pat, don't rub," Beth would always say.

Beth then led me back to the exam room where Dr. Hamburger would see me. The little room had a short bed in the middle, and a machine in the corner that I'd look into while he shined bright lights in my eye. Three chairs lined the wall where my mom, my stepdad Chris, and my dad sat. I was expected to sit up on the exam table, or in one of my parents' laps, but I took my place in the doctor's little rolly chair. When Hamburger came into the room after what seemed like forever, he gave me a stern look signaling that I needed to find a new seat, so I took my place in Mom's lap.

The exam was pretty routine: he sat down, had me take my prosthetic out, washed it, poked his gloved fingers around in my eye socket, gave my eye back to me and watched me put it in, examined my left eye, muttered to himself, wrote in his book, then scooted the rolly chair back so that he could see all of us. Dr. Hamburger then said some things to us. I didn't understand the words he was using, but I saw Mom break down sobbing. Dr. Hamburger, my mom, and my stepdad got up and went into a separate room, and I sat there with my dad. He crouched down on the floor in front of me.

"Daddy, what's wrong with Mommy?" I asked.

"Mommy is just sad, sweetie. Your cancer came back. Do you know what that means?" he asked. I couldn't see well enough to say what his face looked like. But his voice sounded sad. Seeing and hearing my parents' reactions frightened me. They were always strong and happy, and I'd never seen them so upset, especially not at a simple check-up. I responded to his question by bringing my hand up to my eye. At the time, I didn't know much about cancer, except that it was why I couldn't see.

My mom came back into the room with a smile on her face. She sat down and pulled me back into her lap. My parents talked to Hamburger a while longer, and they decided to go ahead and do an MRI that day. I refused to lie down or go into the machine. They tried bribing me with a baby doll of my favorite Disney princess, Belle, but I wouldn't budge. Finally, my dad volunteered to go into the machine first to show me that it really wasn't that scary, and that I would not get eaten by the MRI.

All summer, Mom drove me to Louisville, two hours up and two hours back every single weekday, just to sit in a waiting room for ten minutes while I got my radiation treatments. I hated the car ride, but I loved the treatment because of the hot doctor who would always give me a piggy back ride back to the radiation room. Mom couldn't go back with me. Even the doctors and nurses couldn't be in the radiation room. Just me, the giant machine, a CD player full of my favorite Disney princess songs, and the smell of burning flesh—like a dying animal—that accompanied the treatment. After my last treatment, everyone was full of joy and celebrated, especially my mom. I pouted because I didn't get to say goodbye to the hot doctor, who had that day off.

I know that it hurt my mom to see me go through all the treatments when I was so young. She had times when she broke down, but that's because she's human. You can only hold on for so long before it all bursts like a dam. But most of the time she was the strong one. When my dad didn't want to change my eye bandages because he didn't want me to hate him, my mom did it, even though she passed out the first time. When someone had to be tough and do the things that were best for me, she was the one who did them.

My two full blooded sisters are Larrissa and Brooklyn. Larrissa is the eldest, four years older than me, and Brooklyn is two years younger than me. We had another sister, Veronica Hancock Loyd, who was stillborn. We have a box that is probably the same size Veronica was, where we keep things to remind us of her. Sometimes I like to go through it just so I feel a little closer to the sister I never met. There's a white blanket with a bloody spot that has faded over time, newspaper articles honoring her death, and little notes my mom has written for her. We've all written letters to her on her major birthdays, and vowed to open and read them when she would have turned twenty-one. There are also pictures of her lifeless body, the one time that mother and child met. It is a very sad thought for me, and I can only imagine how my mom must have felt.

The day that my mom found out that she was pregnant with my little sister Brooklyn was also the day she found out that I had cancer. My older sister tells me that I can't ever let anyone else have the attention—even as a baby, I couldn't let Brooklyn have her shining moment with Mom, because my cancer became the focus of everything.

Each of us girls has our different roles. Larrissa is the control freak, mother hen, and responsible sister. Brooklyn is the laid back, go-with-the-flow, easy-to-please, gets-into-everything, and never-listens sister. I am the strong headed, loud, mean, controlling diva. Larrissa and Brooklyn have always been more reserved and usually don't speak

The day that my mom found out that she was pregnant with my little sister Brooklyn was also the day she found out that I had cancer.

Photos courtesy of Madelyn Loyd

their minds, so I've made it my own personal duty to defend them, and make sure that they are heard.

I remember the first time that I really stood up for one of my sisters. The summer after my first grade year, Larissa and I were shipped off to day camp. I hated it and spent the majority of my day crying to go home. A bunch of older girls were being really mean to Larissa. She came out of her class crying and told me, "Maddy, I really just want to go home. The girls in there are calling me a liar because I told them you had a fake eye, and they keep calling me names and picking on me."

I marched up to that classroom and slammed the door open. I was scared, because I was just going into the second grade, and these girls were a lot bigger than me, but I wasn't going to let anyone talk to my sister that way and make her cry.

"Hey!" I shouted, "I don't know who you guys think you are, but my sister is not a liar! If you need proof, I can take my eye out right now, but if you throw up, it's your own fault. Be nice to my sister!"

Most people consider me to be a very strong, outgoing individual, and for the most part I am. I'm a people person, and I love socializing. Although I can be outspoken, a lot of people who know me now find it hard to believe that I have not always been this way. There was a time in school when I'd just sit quietly and watch everything unfold. I let people say what they wanted to about me, and avoided any situation that could turn ugly.

I never raised my hand in class. I could answer most questions, but when a teacher just points instead of saying names, how is the blind girl to know who's being called on? I learned that lesson after many times of sitting there with my hand in the air while other kids just stared at me. The teacher would finally realize her mistake, and I would give my answer with a face as red as my hair. I didn't even speak up for things that I needed

Photo courtesy of Madelyn Loyd

because I felt like a burden to my teachers already. All of the other kids in my class were fine on their own; they didn't need any fancy machines to finish their work. I fumbled my way through and acted like I knew what I was doing. Looking back, I regret a lot of the times that I was afraid to speak up.

I really didn't have any friends until the second grade. I was afraid to talk to people, so I always waited for other people to talk to me first. I was self-conscious because I couldn't tell if I looked different from the other kids. Sometimes I'd respond to someone only to find out they weren't talking to me at all. All of this made me a pretty miserable child at school, and there were many mornings when I would come in crying for my mom and pretend to get sick so that the nurse would have to send me home. I hated school, hated not being at home, hated being thrown into a place where I couldn't rely on anyone but some teacher I didn't know. How was I supposed to trust and tell all of my problems to someone I didn't know any better than a stranger at the store? It was scary for me. I felt like I was stuck all by myself. The only relief in my school day was when I got to go with my vision teacher, Mrs. Kaye. She was my only friend in elementary school for a long time. I knew I could trust her, and she became like a second mother or a grandmother to me.

A vision teacher helps blind or visually impaired students learn braille, stay organized, address special accommodations, and write the student's Individual Education Plan. But to some students, like me, a vision teacher becomes more like a friend. I first met Kaye Daugherty in preschool when all I really wanted was to be like the other kids. But while they were doing art or playing with toys, I was taken to a little room with Mrs. Kaye to learn the things a visually impaired kid needs to know. She was strict, and always seemed to show up right when I was doing something to make her unhappy. I hated her at first, and hated that she was taking over my life at school.

As I grew older, I started to warm up to Mrs. Kaye, and instead of one of my least favorite people, she became one of my favorites. Unlike new teachers who you meet at the beginning of the year, say goodbye to at the end, and never speak to again, Mrs. Kaye was always there, every year. She was a constant in my life, which was very comforting.

Of course, there were times when I wished Mrs. Kaye would just leave me alone, like the day in third grade when she sat me down with my backpack and told me that we were going to organize everything. Organization had become a big thing with her, but I was not interested; I was more than happy to continue shoving my papers into my backpack and never seeing them again. I got a bad attitude with her, and I was furious that she was going through my things. We got into a huge fight that had me in tears. I was so angry. There were a couple of days like this, where we would spend the whole class time yelling and arguing with each other.

I spent my sixth grade year trying my hardest to test her and give her the worst attitude I could muster. I hated braille. I hated that I had extra homework that other kids didn't. I hated that I had to work three times as hard as everyone else just to stay on track. I thought Mrs. Kaye was the one to blame. She was the one pulling me from class, giving me extra homework, pushing me to be the very best, and I despised her for that. Looking back now, I know that she was trying to help me. Thanks to Mrs. Kaye, I was extremely successful in middle school, and everything she has taught me has led to my success and achievements now. Without her, I would have stayed in my shell, never had any friends, never participated in anything.

When Mrs. Kaye announced her retirement, it was time for me to do some hard thinking. I was already worried about going to high school. Every kid is. But I was concerned about losing my friends who were accustomed to my blindness and knew what I needed help with. I was worried about not being able to find my classes in such a large, confusing building, or not being able to see where to go in the cafeteria to get my lunch. All of these things would be easy for me to handle now because I've learned to be more independent and advocate for myself. At the time, though, I was too worried about fitting in and not needing any "special" help. Most of all, I was worried about having a new vision teacher. I had been with Mrs. Kaye since preschool, and now, in the biggest transition of my teenage life, she wasn't going to be there.

I'd thought about the Kentucky School for the Blind before, but it hadn't seemed necessary. As time progressed, and my anxiety about high school grew, I knew that I needed to go. I knew I was leaning too heavily on everyone around me at home and that I had to learn some independence to grow. When I presented the idea to my mom, I could tell she wasn't too crazy about my being so far away, but she stood behind me. She knew as well as I did that it would be the best move. I took a blind leap of faith and made up my mind to go to KSB.

In 2013, I moved two hours away from home to the Kentucky School for the Blind in Louisville. I knew that there wasn't any school in Kentucky that would be more beneficial for me, but sometimes it was really hard. I've always been a homebody, so having to stay in Louisville all week long could be really trying for me. But I loved being at KSB, where I got to know so many great people and learned so much about independence, love, and individuality.

I lived in the independent high school dorm for two years. This meant that my roommate and I were in charge of everything: we cooked, cleaned, did our own laundry, got ourselves up in the morning, shopped for groceries and did almost anything else that independence entails. Chip and Lauren, our dorm parents, were in charge of the independent dorm. They were cool, more like mentors or friends than supervisors. Sometimes we'd go sit and chat in their office when we were bored. They helped us when we cooked, make sure that we cleaned everything, and taught us independent living skills.

I have always had a wonderful, caring family, through good times and hard times. No matter how tough things get, I always have people around who love and support me. That's something I really appreciate, because I am at a huge turning point in my life. In the fall of 2015, I found out that I was pregnant and that I was going to have a baby in June of 2016. My pregnancy was definitely earlier in life than what I planned or expected, but I would never have had it any other way, and my family couldn't have been any more supportive, my mom especially. I'm not sure what it was about being pregnant that made me so clingy to my mom, but all I wanted was to be home with her and my family.

The school counselor and my mom determined that I should continue attending KSB until my third trimester began. I'd come home for good around spring break. Things were difficult, though. I was still a teenager, still in school, still visually impaired, living in dorms with my peers two hours away from my family and my home. Sunday through Tuesday were the worst: I'd beg my mom to please come get me, was comforted by my wonderful boyfriend, Shane, and told by teachers that I'd be fine. By Wednesday, I'd accept that I needed to be at KSB, and hoped that time would fly by like everyone claimed it would. On Fridays I'd go back home and be fine again. Come Saturday I'd be begging my mom not to make me go back. The same pattern every week. It was miserable. I couldn't take it anymore. I couldn't stand being depressed all of the time. I felt cold and empty at KSB, like all of the blood was drained from my chest and replaced by ice.

I didn't stay through spring break. I left KSB for good in early January. It was an abrupt decision. Not everything was planned out. I didn't know how it would all work out from that point on. Would I go back to public school in Owensboro? I definitely didn't want to; it is hard enough starting someplace new where you don't have any friends, but it's even worse when your first impression on everyone is that you are seventeen and pregnant. A lot of people can be really cruel about that stuff, and I was afraid I would be an immediate target. Add a disability into the mix, and you have a bunch of high school students staring at your pregnant belly or your white cane. My social life would be doomed if I had to go back to public school in Owensboro, so I started online correspondence courses, which have been stressful; I perform best with a lot of structure, and it is important for me to have a clear schedule. I know the program is what's best for my future, so I have to be a big girl and deal with it.

I have learned a lot in these past few months, not only from the situation I am in, but from the people around me, the choices I've made, and the opportunities I've had. Everything is a little bittersweet. I don't see my KSB friends anymore, but I get my own little family. I miss being around everyone at KSB, but I'm so excited about what is to come. I don't regret my choices at all, and I've had my eyes opened to many things. I've realized that it is important to be your own person.

It's hard enough starting someplace new, but it's even worse when your first impression on everyone is that you're seventeen and pregnant.

Photo courtesy of Madelyn Loyd

I was pretty immature when I was at KSB, and I had an awful attitude problem. I acted differently depending on who I was with, and I know now that it was a cry for attention. I wanted to be someone who people wanted to be around, someone who made people laugh, someone who people noticed. So many times when I was in public school, I was the outcast, the one who the popular kids would be rude to or hate for no reason. At KSB, I was the one who was rude to people. More and more, I hated the person I was becoming.

When I got with Shane, I decided that I wanted to show him who I really was, not who I pretended to be to everyone else, and I'm so glad I did. I finally had someone who knew me, knew how I really felt. He encouraged me to be the real me. When I got pregnant, things really got put into perspective for me. I didn't want to act the way I had in the past. I had focused so heavily on how people thought of me that I had neglected to really connect with the people who I could have become really close to. By the time I left KSB, I was more confident that people knew who I really was.

I have lots of good memories with people from KSB, and I still love everyone there. I miss all of the times with my best friend, Kianna. I miss late nights hanging out in Chip's office with the independent dorm crew, socializing with everyone at rec, sneaking out of my dorm at night to go tell Kianna a funny story, to try to scare her, or to borrow a hairbrush, which I often misplaced. I will always remember my experiences at KSB, and the people I grew to love, but I know that it is time to embrace what is coming next. I have Shane, my family, and my son, and I feel pretty blessed.

After much harassment from my mother, who was absolutely desperate to start ordering embroidered things, Shane and I decided on a name: our son would be named Kayson Oliver Lowe. Kayson is a Greek name that means *healer*. The middle name Oliver means *dignity, beauty, and peace*. The last name Lowe means *little wolf*. We think it is a good, meaningful, strong name, and we think it's pretty cute.

Every expecting mother has her fears and concerns, and I've been no exception. One of my biggest fears is that my mothering will be judged and ridiculed by sighted people. As a visually impaired parent, I know that I will do things differently from most people. Simple tasks like getting the baby dressed, changing his diaper, and bathing him, are things people use their vision to do without even thinking of it. But Shane and I can't rely on sight. We'll have to do things in a way that is better for us and gets the job done more efficiently. My worry is that people will tell us that we are doing it all wrong. The way we do certain things may be slower than if a sighted person were doing them, but we have to take care of our child. If it ends up taking longer, so what?

I also worry that other parents will think I'm weird because I can't just let my child run around while I sit somewhere and watch from a distance. I'll have to be down on the floor with Kayson, following him around because I won't be able to see what he is doing from a distance. If he were to put some random object in his mouth, I wouldn't be able to see it, and I don't want him getting hurt. My job is to make sure he's safe. Some parents may think I'm hovering or overbearing, but I'll just be ensuring my child's safety the best way I know how.

I am also worried about still living with my family while Kayson is a baby. I know I will need and appreciate any help they give us, but I'm afraid that my parents may step in too much, and I really want to be as independent as I can when it comes to raising Kayson. I know I'm going to have some hardships and setbacks, but that won't stop me from being the best mom I can be. Mom says that every new mother does things differently, and that it's important that I don't let what others think change what I believe is best for my son. She's shown me that being a mother isn't just cuddling a cute baby, it's dealing with all of the hard, unpleasant things too, like changing diapers, dealing with bad moods, having to clean up after the baby, having to make the hard decisions about medical situations. But most of all, my mother has taught me pure, unconditional love. Just by the way she treats my sisters and me, she has shown me true compassion and understanding. Being a mom is going to be hard, but I have seen just how rewarding that job can be, and I hope to be as great as my mom is.

The surgeon said not to eat past 8:00 PM in case I ended up needing a C-section, so the night before I was induced, Mom and Chris took the family out to dinner at Cheddars as a celebration, or a sort of last meal before Kayson arrived. All of the worry and anticipation had finally set in, and I was not in a very good mood. I just wanted to be at home in the solitude of my bedroom. Shane was nervous and tired too. Everyone else was in a great mood and excited. Mom wanted to keep taking pictures, and I didn't want to have any part in it. I just wanted to eat my chicken sandwich, go home, go to bed, and get the next day started so that I wouldn't have to worry about it anymore.

I didn't go to sleep at all, though; I was too excited and anxious. I stayed up, lurking around on Facebook, reading articles on childbirth, watching YouTube videos about coping with contraction pain, trying my very best to be prepared. I had been so ready to meet my son, I had convinced myself that I wasn't going to freak out when the time came, but as we got closer to inducing, I found myself plotting out everything that could go wrong. I have super bad luck, and I had convinced myself that life was working against me. I was so worried that I had made it this far only to have a stillbirth. Or perhaps the epidural would go wrong and I would find myself paralyzed. My anxiety attack started at dinner, and I wasn't scheduled to be induced until 4:00 in the morning. By the time we pulled into the hospital parking lot, my anxiety was so intense I thought I'd pass out before we even made it through the door.

We were taken to the room where I'd give birth to my son. The room was big, with a bed in the middle, a recliner and a couch for my family, and an area where they would clean Kayson up after he was born. I dimmed the lights, hoping I could get a little sleep. The nurse took my pulse and placed a blood pressure cuff on my right arm. She went to put an IV in my left arm but said my veins weren't impressing her. She fetched a warm blanket to wrap around my arm to hopefully cause some of my veins to show; that heated blanket was one of my favorite parts of the hospital. I finally got an IV in, and they started me on Pitocin, a medication used to induce labor, which helped things progress immediately. I don't exactly know how to describe the feeling of having a contraction; it felt like my insides were squeezing in on themselves. It was painful.

I laid there in the room with my mom and Shane and attempted to get some sleep. I wasn't really in the talking mood, so I just laid there and relaxed as much as I could. Mom and Shane talked to one another. Shane also had a good book that he was reading while I slept, and Mom watched me, or was on her phone. It seemed like every time I managed to fall asleep, Kayson would move away from the heart rate monitor, and the nurse would have to come back in to find him again. Once Pitocin was started, it took about seven hours for me to progress enough for them to break my water.

I knew the epidural needle would be enormous and that I'd have to sit really still while they were doing it. I was terrified that something would go wrong, so scared that I started to cry. When the nurse told me that only one person could stay with me while I got the shot, I looked over at Shane and told him I was sorry, but that I just really needed my mom. He was fine with my decision and left me and Mom together.

I was contracting painfully. The anesthesiologist asked me sit up with my legs crossed on the bed and bend over. My mom and the nurse were holding onto me as I was hunched over, my back arched like a cat. Then the anesthesiologist put the epidural into my back. She said I'd feel a sharp pain, which was the numbing medicine, and that this would be the worst part. I immediately started bawling my eyes out. It was the worst feeling I'd ever felt, like something alien being put into my body, something that just didn't belong, like somebody shoving a shelf into my spine.

The contraction pains stopped, but the pressure I was feeling in my bum was so uncomfortable, like a leg was poking into it. I told my mom to get the nurse because the pressure was starting to be way too much to handle. I went from five centimeters dilated to ten in less than forty minutes. The nurses scrambled to prepare the table for my delivery and they let me push a little to relieve the pressure. Shane and Mom were both at my side, and Mom noticed that I was already bleeding a lot. She asked the nurses if I was OK. They told her that I'd torn a little bit, and that we really needed Dr. Dawson to get there. Later I was told that they lost Kayson's heartbeat for a minute, a detail I'm glad that I didn't know at the time.

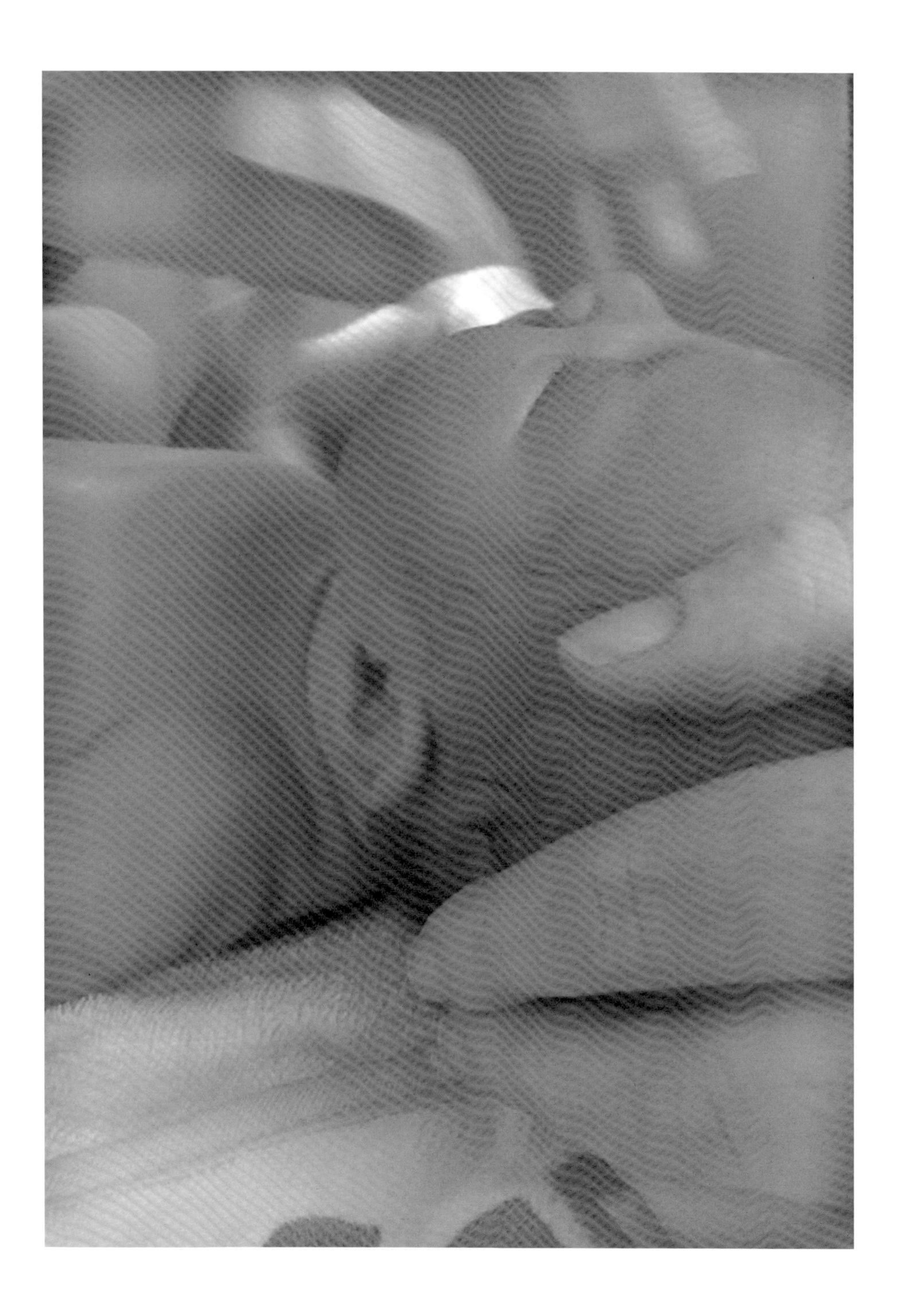

Photo courtesy of Madelyn Loyd

All the complications of pregnancy, the stress, the responsibility, the pain of birth: it was all worth it.

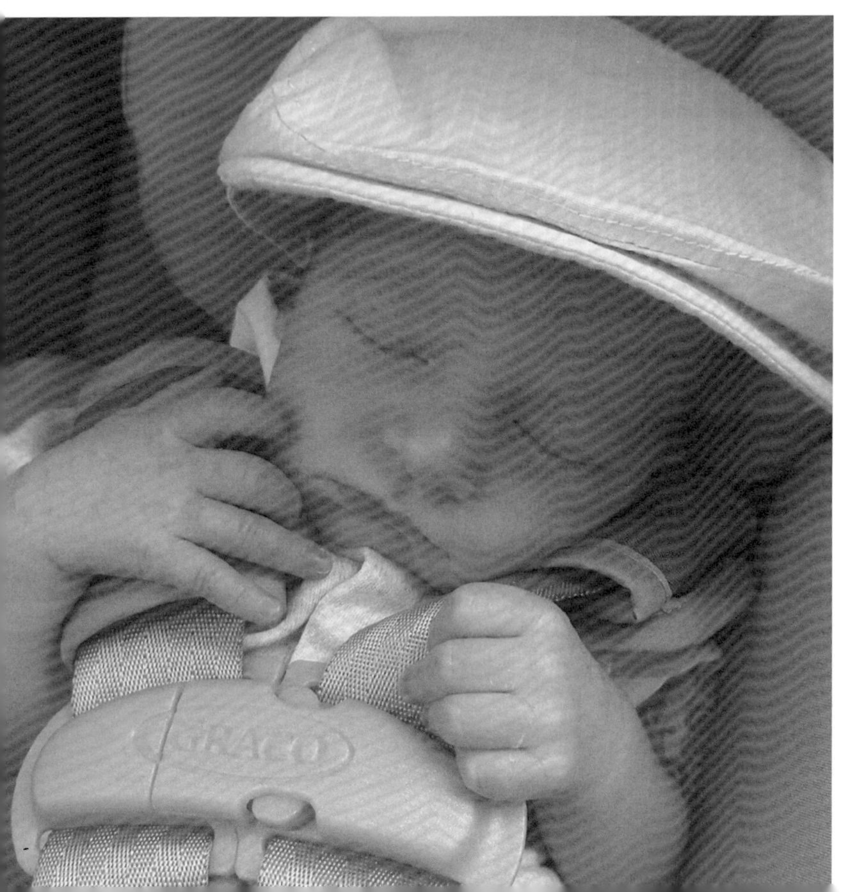

Photos courtesy of Madelyn Loyd

I started pushing for real when the doctor arrived, and Kayson Oliver Lowe was born at 5:59 PM on May 24. They immediately put him on my chest, and I was in love. He was perfect. I started talking to him, telling him how happy I was that he was here, and how much I loved him. I didn't know anything that was going on around me—I was too focused on Kayson—but Mom tells me that the nurses were rubbing his back, that he was sort of a blue color, and that he wasn't crying. He was only on my chest for a little while before they took him away. My mom came over and told me that they were going to take him to the NICU, and asked me if it was alright if she went back with him. The nurses went too because Kayson wasn't breathing very well. At 9:00 PM I was moved to the mother/baby unit without my baby.

I was terribly worried about Kayson, but I knew in my heart that he would be just fine. I knew that any son of mine would be just as stubborn as me; Kayson would be a fighter. The night before I was induced, when I told her how worried I was, my mom called me a super trooper. So, when she came back from the nursery and said, "Guess who's a super trooper just like his mama?" I knew he was OK, and I have never been more relieved in my life. Then there was a knock on my door. "Nursery!" said a voice. My heart stopped. My baby was finally coming to my room to stay with me. This was the beginning of a lifetime of bonding and love, and I couldn't wait to hold him. The nurse wheeled the little bed over to me and placed my son in my arms. I couldn't stop smiling. I held my son tightly against my chest, knowing that everything I'd been through had led me up to this moment. All the complications of pregnancy, the stress, the responsibility, the pain of birth: it was all worth it. I stroked his cheek and kissed his nose. Shane came over, sat down, and wrapped his arms around us both.

Precious love and pick-up lines

DEBBY HANCOCK

Nana was the first person to help me realize my love of writing. There's still a drawer in the back room of her house full of little stapled booklets of my poems. Writing with Nana is one of my favorite memories. We've always shared a special bond, like I'm a smaller version of her. She is a beautiful, strong, independent individual. I have always felt connected to her. Still, every time I talk with her, we discover something new that we have in common. Now that I'm older, I appreciate her even more. She is a wonderful woman, and I'm proud to call her my Nana.

My name is Debby Hancock. I was born June 2, 1957 here in Owensboro, Kentucky at the Lady of Mercy Hospital. I have ten brothers and two sisters. Two brothers and one sister are dead now. I was the oldest girl, so there were a lot of things I had to do around the house. It was a lot of fun having that many siblings. Some of them bonded with me almost like I was their mom. It was a wild ride.

My parents were very hard workers. Dad was a contractor and oversaw the construction of a lot of houses. He had a lot of employees under him. Mom worked at General Electric Company making little tubes for TVs and things like that, but the babysitters were not always as kind to us as she expected, so she wound up a stay-at-home mom. She was very busy with a lot of cooking, a lot of laundry. When Dad came home, he would get all of the things ready for the next day on the jobsite, then he would

Photo courtesy of Debby Hancock

come in and help Mom cook meals. He was an army cook, so he enjoyed cooking dinner and getting up and making us breakfast. So we saw him a lot. Dad loved us being right there. Dad also grew tobacco, so I'd also help out in the fields sometimes, weeding and hoeing the tobacco.

I lived in a lot of homes growing up. At that time, when you were a contractor like Dad, homes sold better if someone was living in them. We would live in the houses for so long, Dad would sell them, then we would move to the next home he was building. As time went on, it got to where you could build the homes and sell them without having to live in them, but in the beginning we moved quite a bit. Mom did all the decorating, all the color scheme and everything. We had a lot of the amenities that some people in that time did not have: a dishwasher and always a good washer and dryer and things like that. Even though we usually had a big house we didn't all have our own room. I can remember one house we were living in. It only had four bedrooms, and there were twelve of us.

The best house that we lived in growing up was on South Hampton Road. We had lots of family who would come and stay all night with us and bring their kids. Dad had built us a playhouse behind our house up on a hill. Me being the only girl for so long, I played with a lot of boys. I wasn't a tomboy, but I played cowboys and Indians more than I played with baby dolls. A lot of times when all of the cousins would come down we would all pitch up tents and go and stay all night and have fires. Those were some super fun times. We had our bikes so we were able to ride back on the lanes. We grew up going outside and throwing dirt clods at each other. We knew that you could just go jump in the lake and wash it all off.

I see my family all the time. They all live here in Owensboro or in Frankfort, and we see each other quite often. I go to my mom's at least three or four times a week and talk with her almost every day. We all are still a very tight, close family. My dad passed away in May. That was one experience that I don't think I'll ever forget; I think it brought us even closer as a family.

I left home when I was eighteen and was staying with a friend. I met your Papaw one night when I was sitting outside on the porch by myself playing my guitar. He stopped by and saw me on the porch and said, "Hey, do you remember me?" He'd passed through my friend's house before. I said, "Yeah, I remember you." He said, "Well, I had a gig in Florida and my guitar is still with the band. You don't mind if I grab your guitar and play a tune, do you?"

So he played a tune, and I thought, *Wow, he's a really great singer and really great guitar player*. Then he said, "I'm getting ready to go over to some friends' house and I don't have my guitar because it's still in Florida. Can I borrow your guitar?" It's like, *OK, what kind of a pickup line is this?* So I said, "I'll tell you what, you can borrow my guitar as long as you take me with you." I totally fell in love with him that night and knew that God had sent him to me and that he was the one that was meant for me. That was August 31 of 1975, and we married on December 13 of 1975. We've been married for forty years. Our whole life has been a time of growing closer and closer. I guess it was meant to be.

Being the oldest girl of my siblings, I've always been the mother type, so at eighteen years old I was ready to have kids and be settled down. Your mother Brandy was born in September of 1976, then Daniel was born in June of 1977—he was very premature—and then Charlie came ten months later. So when me and your Pops would go out, people thought I had triplets. All of the babies were small in stature and redheads. They really looked a lot alike, and there was not a lot of difference in height and everything.

We taught your mom and your uncles to sing from a very early age. I love music. Contemporary liturgical and country are what I sing the most. I sing with my brothers at church from time to time. I sing with your pops, and he's into more of your country type of music. When Pops and I were in the ministry, we recorded a country gospel CD. We did a lot of traveling and singing across several different states. We'd hook up the camper and go from church to church, city to city, and state to state. He would preach and we would sing together. We would have the kids singing right along with us.

I can't say that it was easy, but it wasn't hard either. I loved that time. Really I think the only reason that we ever came back to Owensboro and settled down is because as

Photo courtesy of Madelyn Loyd

the kids got older we got to thinking, *If we're here and we're here and we're here and they meet a boyfriend or a girlfriend as they get older, will they wind up maybe staying in another state?* I wanted them close to me.

My relationships with my kids are pretty good. I'm very close to my daughter. I love her with all my heart. She's everything to me. My sons I'm not quite as close with. They have experienced a lot of life. In their teenage years they got into the drug scene, and so I think addiction caused us not to be as close. But they are finally really growing up and are overcoming the addiction. I give the Lord all the praise for that. The more they are in recovery, the closer they become to Him.

I was in early childhood education for sixteen or seventeen years. After we closed the day care, I switched gears and started at the bank. Then your mother had you, and you were diagnosed with the retinoblastoma. I started working at McDonald's part time because they allowed me to work the hours that I wanted to work, and if you got sick I was able to leave work immediately. If your mom called me and said, "Hey, Maddy is sick, we need to take her to Cincinnati immediately, she's running a fever," I could leave. Now I am a catering coordinator for Great Harvest, and I love my job. I love getting up and going to work in the morning.

I love life. Life is so precious. You should love everyone, find the good in everyone. If you read anything about Mother Teresa or Gandhi, that's what their whole thing is about: loving all. Just be happy and share kindness, share love, share happiness. We don't ever know what anyone is going through, so if someone comes into work and they're crabby and they're hateful, there are a lot of times that I'll just give that person a hug and tell them, "Have a great day. I love you." There are a lot of people who will stop in just to have me give them a hug because they say that it makes their day when they see me smile. That's what life is all about. It's not hard to give kindness or a smile away, and you don't know what you're doing for that other person when you do. You might be changing that person's whole life.

Photo by Jessica Ebelhar

Photo by Jessica Ebelhar

MATTHEW CAUDILL

Matthew Caudill

FROM THE MOUNTAIN TO SELF-RELIANCE

The leaves were still green, but a cold wind was blowing. I stared out the window of the school bus at the mountains of Perry County, Kentucky, which dropped down into the bottoms and the flatlands on the other side in the valley. Back in Middle's Fork, we passed my aunt's house where the road is elevated. Everything on her property was built by my great grandfather Otis. I saw her white home, her oval driveway with the garden in the middle, the woodworking building, a garage out back, a barn, and an old pigpen, but there are no pigs in it any more.

My sister tried to get my attention because it was time to get off the bus, but all of a sudden I couldn't move. I could think, and see, and I could hear my sister talking to me, telling me over and over that it was time to get off the bus, but I couldn't move. I was just staring at my aunt's house down the hill from the road. My sister started shaking me, but I couldn't respond. Then nothing—blackness—like when you are about to wake up from a dream.

Then there were people I didn't know standing over me asking if I was OK. I was confused and then was bombarded by hugs from my mother and my grandmother. As the paramedics helped me up, they asked me if I wanted to ride in an ambulance. I told them no, that I wanted to ride with people I know, so my mom drove us to the hospital in my granny's tiny blue car. They were constantly asking me if I was OK on the way to the hospital. When we got there, I was put in my own room, and I was surrounded by my family. The doctors checked me out to see what had happened, and they found out that the blood had stopped going to my brain because I'd had another seizure. I'd had them before, I guess, but this was the first one I remember, and it was scary. They did what they could do to see how I was doing, but said that I needed to go all the way to Cincinnati to have some tests done. We drove up there five times for CT scans and MRIs. Once, when I was asleep in the car on the way to Cincinnati, my parents kept seeing rainbows. My dad told my mom that it was a good sign, and everything was going to be all right.

The catalyst for the seizures that damaged part of my brain was an allergic reaction to the pertussis vaccine in my booster shots when I was a baby. My problems didn't manifest until I was in first grade when the damage to my occipital lobe resulted in some vision loss. My mom and dad took me to go get my eyes checked out; 20/180 is not legally blind, but almost there. I have to be twenty feet away to see something you could see from 180 feet. So, I'm vanilla blind, which means I look like I'm sighted even though I'm not part of the sighted community. I can exist in both worlds and have the support of both groups. Some people think I am completely blind and need to be waited on, and other people think I'm quote-unquote normal. Some people are amazed that I can tie my own shoes, but other times blind stereotypes do not come to people's minds. One time when I was using my cane, some guy said, "I will pray for you, my brother." I'd had people pray for me before, but only when I was sick. It was strange, to say the least. I did not need him to pray for me. I am not that blind, but it's nice to know that there are people out there who will pray for you.

I have a lot of freedom in my life right now. I graduated from the Independent Living Program at the Kentucky School for the Blind, and I will go to college in Indiana after I get my basics at Hazard Community College. I will also be working on getting my bioptic driver's license, which will allow me to drive using a small telescope attached to a pair of glasses. It feels awesome to go where I want when I want now. But I had a pretty sheltered life growing up in Viper, Kentucky. I was kept close and watched by everyone so they could keep me safe. I did not have many friends up there, so we did everything together. I didn't go out much unless it was with them. Because of this, I am very close to my mom and dad, and my big sister Brittany, and I wouldn't change anything even if I could.

My mom and I are very close. If not for her, I wouldn't be who I am today, and I would not be saved in Christ right now. She is the reason I found Christ, but I'm not evangelist about it. I have lived here my whole life, and I found God here in Hazard. My papaw Carl was a preacher at Logwood Church of Christ, and we went there until my mom was invited to go to New Hope. I was in Sunday school there for a year, and my sister had her wedding there. Then my mom was invited to Summit non-denominational, which meets inside the Forum Theater in Hazard because that's the only place big enough to hold that many people. Summit rents the theater on Sundays. They have black and red chairs that make a checkerboard pattern and a band with a few singers. They only sing hymns when the pastor is teaching a lesson. Mostly they play new Christian songs that are out on the radio. They project the lyrics on a screen so people can sing along, which I do. 800 people come on Easter services in the afternoon, and there were 1000 people for two sermons on Christmas. Summit is the church where I was saved.

One Sunday, Pastor Mark said, "If you all want to give your life to Jesus, please bow your heads and pray with me." All heads were bowed and all eyes closed. With his booming voice he led the prayer: *Dear Jesus, forgive me for my sins. Come into my life and save me. I want you to be my Lord. Thank you for loving me and saving me. Help me to live for you from this moment forward. In Jesus' name Amen*. "If you prayed then raise your hand," he said. I turned to my mom and with a shaking voice told her that I prayed the prayer to Jesus and that the light was in me. She hugged me with a big grin on her face. As everybody left, me and my mom caught our pastor.

I was kept close
and watched by
everyone so they could
keep me safe.

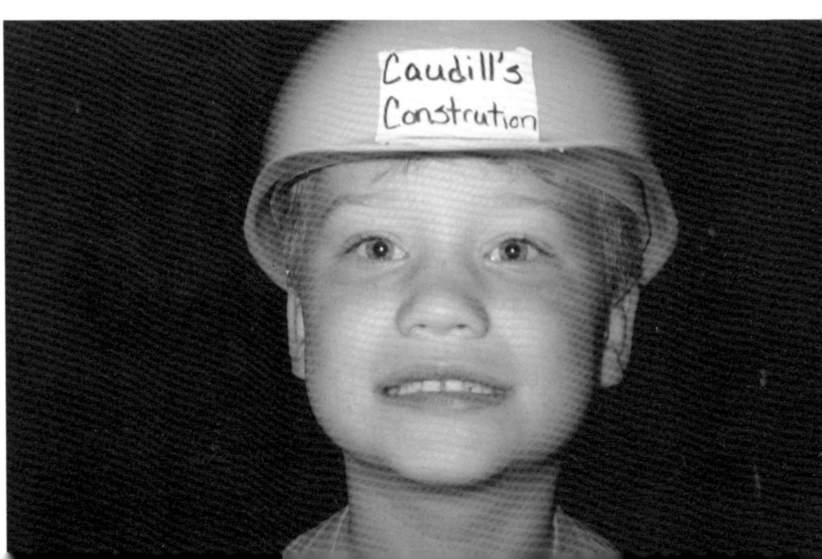

Photos courtesy of the Caudill family

"Mark, Matthew has something to say." Mom told him.

Mark turned and looked at me. He's a skinny man, a huge Star Wars nerd, and always wears a plaid shirt. He's the kind of man who's easy to talk too, but I was still nervous.

"I gave my life to Christ," I said. He smiled, and shook my hand.

"Thank you for sharing this important news with me. This is an important step in your life with Christ. We'll make arrangements for your baptism."

At my grandfather's church, they believe that when you give your life to Christ, you get baptized right then and there on the spot. At Summit they have to bring in the baptistery, so we scheduled my baptism. My family was there that great day. My mom was so proud of me when it was finally my turn.

"Do you, Brother Matthew, give your life to God, Jesus, and the Holy Ghost?" I said, "Yes!" very loudly, my voice booming like I was using megaphone. I felt so free. It was amazing. I thanked Mom for being with me, and God for saving me.

Now we go to a new church, Journey Christian Church. It is a hundred years old and has original wooden pews and an old fashioned piano. I like the way it looks, but Journey has one problem: the music is too loud for my nephews when my sister brings them. Other than that, I am happy with Journey Christian Church.

RAIN

I love the sound of rain. Not just the little rain storms, but the mighty thunder storm. When I would stay the night with my granny Jan and my papa Richard, I liked to go out and sit on their porch in the white, plastic lawn chairs or lean against the rail when it rained. I loved it. You could say my love for rain runs in the family. The rain gives me time to think. Sometimes I will stay out there, daring the thunder. My granny and papa's house is on a hill. When I am up there, I am closer to the heavens above. The dark clouds lighted by moonlight and the dark blue sky—almost, but not quite, black—is a beautiful image.

Photo by Matthew Caudill

Once, when I was a little kid, I asked why Viper is called Viper. "Because somebody killed a snake here once," I was told. It's still funny to me. The pure randomness of it. Viper is where my family has lived for generations. The Caudills came to Kentucky from Ireland and eventually came through the Cumberland Gap with Daniel Boone. They have been noble men, and men of God, preachers who led the church and made their own congregations. I'm proud to be a part of my family. Up the mountain from our house is the Caudill family cemetery. Some of the gravestones there are just rocks, about the size of a head, with writing carved into them that is illegible now. There's a gazebo in honor of the veterans and a shelter with wooden church pews and a podium where we have funerals and family reunions. People come all the way from Ohio and Florida. We cook out and talk. People auction off quilts that they've made, and the money raised goes to keep up the cemetery.

Our house is nestled in a valley with some very tall mountains on either side down by a creek called Field's Fork. We have a big yard, a garden, a barn, and a shed where my dad hangs deer skins. As you wind and curve down the road, pines and poplars provide shade as you pass farms. If you go past my home, it takes you up to my great-great-uncle Corb's house, and past that is a road to one of the strip mines. Everybody takes that way to get to the four-wheeler trails. You will see the lack of trees, dirt everywhere, rocks, and the paths from bulldozers. A strip mine is when they take the top off of a mountain to get to the coal, layer by layer. It's a flat, very dusty mountain. So dusty that they have to put water on the road to keep the dust down when they're working. When they are finished taking the coal, they replant trees.

At the base of the mountain near our house, you will find a cow farm separated by a small stream. It doesn't really have a name; everybody just calls it Duck's Farm. I think he should just hang up a sign and call it that. By the road just past the cows is the underground coal mine that is closed now. That's where my dad used to work for years, and our house used to be right next to the mine before we moved. When I was a baby, the mine moved in right next door, and the TNT kept waking me up and making me cry. The windows would shake, and the noise was like thunder. The mining company paid for us to move back into the holler where we live today.

There is a shirt that my dad has that says, "Coal keeps the lights on." It has a picture of a coal miner standing with his miner's lamp, shining a light. I believe that saying is absolutely true. You need to know this: coal mining was the lifeblood of Perry County for a very long time. When someone finishes high school, they have three paths. Most likely they will be in the coal mines, work in a grocery or another store, or work in the medical field like my mom, who is a surgeon's assistant. It was devastating when the coal mines started laying people off. It hurt families who only had one person bringing in an income, making it hard to get by. The coal mining went downhill, and now people are losing their jobs. Losing their homes. A lot of people are heading out of the state to work. People barely scrape by these days.

Dad has been a lumberjack, cutting down trees and taking them down to sawmills. He has also been in a mine seventeen miles long making sure the machines are up and running. He has operated equipment larger than our house, and he drove a truck for years. When my dad was laid off from the mines, he went to work reclaiming and restoring the land. That helped us with the bills, but it was seasonal work. We had to cut back, go out less, and we didn't take a vacation for a while. My dad farmed more and stayed at the house. It was a struggle, but we got by.

Across from my grandparent's barn, there is an old saw mill that was built by my great-grandfather Otis and his sons Forster, Corb, and Boyd, who also built my aunt's house and all the other buildings there. They still mill lumber there sometimes, but not so much anymore. There's a big red barn, two stories high, with an owl painted on the top. It was painted by my Aunt Martha. There's a pigpen attached to the back surrounded by goose fence.

Near the firehouse, which is also where people vote, is Viper Elementary and Middle Schools. It's a white and green, one-story building with some outdoor classrooms. My mom and dad both went there, so did my sister and I. My nephew goes there now. My papa was a teacher when the school first opened in 1964, and he was a school bus driver, too. He taught all subjects, then started teaching more math and English the longer he was there. He taught for many years.

In elementary school, some teachers thought I was more blind than I was. Others didn't realize how bad my vision was. I was very good at adapting. My principal thought that reading would deteriorate my vision even further, and she said that I shouldn't be reading. My mom tried to tell the principal that reading wouldn't make my vision worse, and she was right: my vision has been getting better. Still, I started reading late in school, and the teachers thought I was slow. I was the kid who was a little slow at reading. Until a few years ago, I had a very hard time reading.

Once, when I got into middle school, a teacher made me go up on stage and read a poem, but I was not able to do it. I got a few words, but my eyes got too tired. It was embarrassing. She thought my vision was better than it really was. That day when I got home, I did what every kid my age would do: I told my mom. The next week I had a new teacher, and I was amazed at what a difference one teacher could make.

My mom helped me in school a lot. She took me to the library to get audiobooks, she encouraged me to read, and she was my scribe: I'd tell her what to write and she would write it. In fourth grade I wrote a poem called "My Secret Appalachian Mountains," and my mom did little illustrations for it. I remember coloring them in a church. On the cover she drew some flowers. The next illustration is of my family's hands: my dad's, my mom's, my sister's and mine. Another is of a table with a food on it: turkey with gravy, green beans, mashed potatoes, deviled eggs and four different pies. She drew a tree in a field of flowers looking at a mountain range, blue skies and a yellow sun. The leaves were all different colors for fall.

That poem was put into a book of writing by kids from my school district. It was one of only two poems chosen from my school to be printed in the book. Everyone was very excited. I have done a lot of writing since then, from poetry, to crafting fantasy worlds, to nonfiction books like this one. In a lineup of a hundred people, I guarantee I'd be the only one who uses the writing techniques that I use. When I write, I sound the words out like a lot of people do, but here is where my way differs from the more traditional methods. I have a speech impediment, so 80% of the time, I spell the word incorrectly when I sound it out. What I do next is to type the word into Google and have it read back to me. I make changes if needed and copy and paste it into what I am

The next week I had a
new teacher, and I was
amazed at
what a difference
one teacher could make.

Photo courtesy of the Caudill family

working on. This takes at least twice as long, but it is my way. I have made vast improvements with this method, and because of my reading program. My reading and writing capabilities have improved ten-fold. Compared to when I was younger, my literary sword has been sharpened to a point that is unsurpassed by my old self.

I attended Perry County High School—home of the Perry County Commodores—for two years. Before my first day, my sister told me how to blend into school so I wouldn't be made fun of, how to be cool, and how not to have awkward conversations. "The first day at lunch, find a table to sit at even if you did not talk much at your old school. Do not sit alone," she said. I did find a table to sit at with one person I knew. I stayed mostly quiet, but I did make friends my first year, and I felt cool. They were a little socially awkward like me. We had one of every single kind of nerd: gamer nerd, YouTube nerd, anime nerd, conspiracy nerd, the geek, a drama nerd, etc.

We would discuss things like the NASA space program, and how they are sending the first manned mission to Mars in 2032. This led to a discussion of terraforming, which is when you make another planet like Earth. Then I'd talk about Doctor Who and four-dimensional space, because I find it intriguing. The others thought it was interesting, but my anime nerd friend did not want to hear it unless I had proof of research, so I did some and let them look at it. We had good times together.

Another time, we talked about *The Hunger Games*. We all read the book and liked the theories and the hidden context clues. Like one time Katniss says, "This place used to be called *Appalachia,*" so we proposed that District 12 was in Kentucky. Katniss' dad worked in the coal mines. Her ancestors had already mined them, so they had to dig deeper and deeper. District 12 is the least cared about of all the districts. They don't have much opportunity there, and people from other districts look down on them. They think the people are poor and not educated. Even in *The Hunger Games'* world there are a lot of stereotypes about Kentucky.

GARDEN

We do not sell the food we grow in the garden. We eat it. My dad, mom, papa, and me will raise the garden from the ground up. When it comes time to plant, we mark lines, we till the land, then we plant the crops: corn, tomatoes, potatoes, beans, onions and my favorites, peppers: jalapeños, dragon-cayenne, habaneros, cow-horn. Working in the sunlight and sometimes by moonlight, we water them, weed the garden, and fertilize. Beans twist and snake up wooden poles. Tomatoes wrap around a wire tower. Then it will be time to pick. Some are ready before others. We will can and dehydrate some of the food and use it the whole year.

Photo by Matthew Caudill

There was this one teacher at school who didn't understand me and my vanilla blindness, and I didn't like how he handled it. When he gave an assignment, it would sometimes take me two weeks to get large-print paper so I could see to do the work. He did not say this, but I got the feeling that he thought I was slow. When I needed to do book work, he'd put me with classmates. They were nice about this, but I do think that they were annoyed a little bit. I made it through, but that teacher "helped" me make my choice to leave home, though it was a difficult decision for me. I knew I needed to learn more independence, and Perry County High was not going to teach me that.

I had an outreach consultant named Verna Howell. She was the one who talked with me and my mom about the Kentucky School for the Blind. We all went to a Mexican restaurant called Sazon's to talk about school once. It wasn't that busy, maybe half full; this was before they expanded. I got my favorite dish, the eagle's plate, it has shrimp and chicken with cheese sauce. My mom and Ms. Howell both had the chicken chimichanga. Ms. Howell told us about the differences between KSB and Perry County High. My mom was asking most of the questions, like what the success rate of students is. I didn't know what to ask, so I asked her if they drove four-wheelers there. She chuckled and said that it's in the city, not the country. Then she told me some history about KSB and about the Independent Living Program, where you have an apartment, learn to cook your own food, and live independently.

When we finished dinner, at home, Mom said that she only wants what is best for me. I mulled it over. I was torn. I was debating in my head between KSB or my friends. It would be hard to leave my friends, but I wanted and needed to go someplace where all the teachers were certified to teach students with visual impairments, and I needed to work on my independence. I told my parents I wanted to go to KSB. My dad said he was OK with it if it would help me. My mom recently said that whenever I go off to college, she will have already gotten all her crying done when I left for KSB.

I swallowed the pill, but when I decided that I wanted to enroll at KSB, there were some repercussions. I couldn't find the words to tell my friends. I took the coward's way and did not tell them that I was going away; I didn't know how, and I felt like I

Photo by Joe Manning

Canon
DIGITAL
THE NORTH FACE

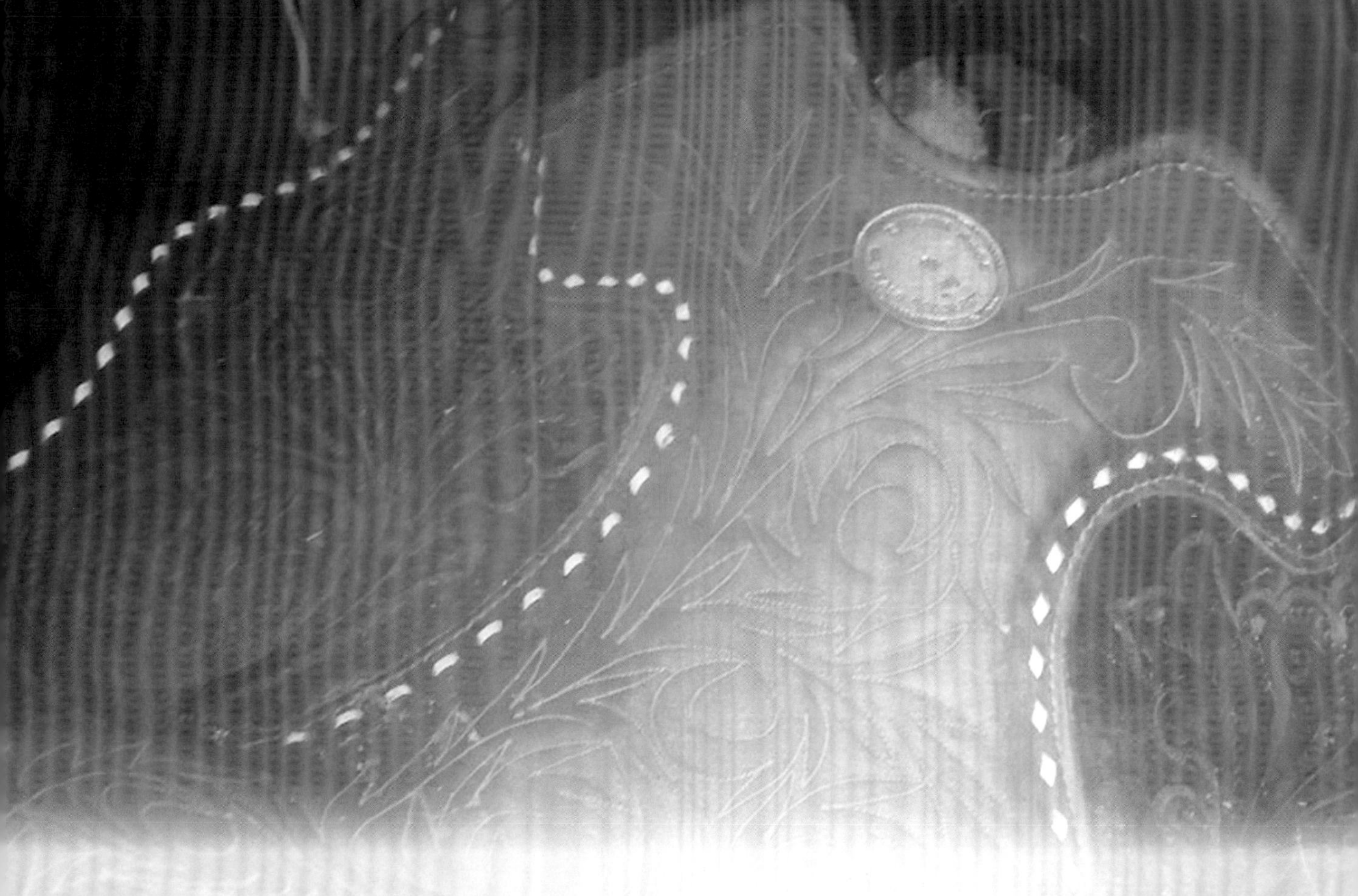

GIFT

Christmas morning, my mom pointed a video camera in my face. I said, "Is it Christmas? I didn't notice it." We opened presents with each other, and later, we stepped outside. Snow coated the ground, and I stared with my sister at our dad who was leading a horse around the yard. We went over to him. His name was Walker. He was a Tennessee Walker. Tall, and brown, with a white diamond on his face. My dad led both of us around, leaving hoof-prints in the snow. The more steps he took, the more prints he left behind. I was ecstatic to pet the horse. He was my sister's, but I still loved how it felt when he ate an apple slice or a sugar cube from my hands. Walker was a good horse.

Photo by Matthew Caudill

betrayed them. When I made it to KSB, my friends and I talked on Skype to each other at night. But before Christmas break one of my friends stopped talking to me. I tried to keep my friendships together, but they were fading away. It was a sad part in my life because I thought I had found friends that would stay with me forever. As they say, the bigger you are the harder you fall.

At KSB I had friends, true friends, and I believe the light of our friendship will not fall into darkness. I learned a lot in the Independent Living Program, like how to pay bills, how to use ATMs, how to plan a budget, and a lot more. Some of the perks were having no stated bedtime, waking up when we wanted to, and cooking our own food, to name a few. Because of Independent Living, I indirectly learned some more social skills: how to deal with problems, and how to live with someone.

When I walked off stage the day of graduation with that diploma in my hand, the world was mine. I'm going to follow the yellow brick road known as the college path. I will stay at my parents' home while I attend Hazard Community and Technical College to get my basics and prerequisites. Then it's off to the Mid-America College of Funeral Service to become a mortician. I will be a good funeral director because I am good with people when they need someone to talk to. I am a good listener because I will actively listen to what you have to say and be there for you. I have talked to my mom about this, and she thinks I will be good at it.

I'd like to get married, own my own funeral home, have a nice yellow car, and live in a big two-story house. It will have four bedrooms, a garage for projects, and somewhere quiet to write fantasy stories in my spare time. I'm not sure where I'll be living, though. I've thought about going to Louisville or Lexington. I have always loved the beach, too. This year's vacation was at Myrtle Beach. One day, I was thinking about what it would be like if I lived there. I asked Cortana, my digital assistant on my phone, "Find a funeral home near me." Lo and behold, there was a funeral home only fifteen minutes away. Living next to the beach, with a short commute to work would be amazing, to say the least. But it would take so long to get back to see everyone, and I wouldn't like that.

Touchdown!

Here on Field's Fork, where I live

LLOYD CAUDILL

My dad is a country man. He was born in a farming family who grew corn, potatoes, tomatoes, and peppers, and raised livestock. He is religious even if he doesn't go to church. My dad is a good man. To some, he is intimidating. He does stuff his own way, and he always get the job done. He loves his home and has no plans to move. He is rooted here in the mountains. He enjoys the simple things in life, like fishing, hunting, going four-wheeler riding or sitting around a big fire just talking for hours. He has worked hard his entire life, from hoeing the garden as a young boy until now. With his salt and pepper hair, sore muscles, joints that pop and crack, he keeps going.

Will you please tell me your name, when and where you were born?

Lloyd Caudill: My name is Lloyd Ernest Caudill. I was born December 6, 1965 in Hazard, Kentucky.

What did you do growing up?

Lloyd Caudill: I played and fished and hunted and worked for my grandpa and my dad. We worked together, hoed corn, cut firewood. Grandpa took me on fishing trips and bought me a rifle one time for hoeing all summer. We fished out of the creek beside the house a lot. We went to the river by Carr's Fork Lake, would catch bluegill. I've caught them thirteen or fourteen inches. We never did measure them. We just caught them and cleaned them

Photo courtesy of the Caudill family

and ate them. We didn't have a whole lot of money. For fun, possum hunting and squirrel hunting and riding motorcycles. My brother, Jimmy Dale, me and him played together all the time. Wasn't but four or five years difference between our age. I was the better hunter. Still am. That was the type of play we did, hunting and fishing. We didn't play games. I played the piano for a couple of years. Miss Angel was my old music teacher when I went to elementary school. I was fair, I could play it. Had a solo at school. We had a piano at home. I haven't played a piano since.

When you were young, did you ever have any chores to do?

Lloyd Caudill: Yes, I did. Every day. Feeding the chickens, cleaning up the yard, cutting firewood, hoeing corn and beans

Did you go to work right after high school?

Lloyd Caudill: Yes, I did. I was a welder and an electrician. Then I went underground in the mines off and on for seven, eight years. I delivered supplies, supported top, and worked on equipment.

How far underground were you usually?

Lloyd Caudill: I don't know, the machine would run eighteen miles an hour on the rail car and it'd take us 45 minutes to get to the place where we were actually mining the coal.

Did you ever do any of the actual mining or did you just repair the machines?

Lloyd Caudill: I did some of the actual mining. It was fine. I didn't have any problem with it. It's hard work and dangerous. I left because I could make the same money working on a strip job or logging or whatever. I went to a strip job. It was good. I ran loaders loading overburden off the top of the coal, loaded coal in the coal trucks, ran bulldozers, escalators, drills. I worked for a contractor, and we'd work at one place a while and then go to another one.

I worked for Nally and Hamilton, Locust Grove, Blackhawk, Shamrock, a whole bunch of companies. Everything I've done in the past thirty years has been coal or logging. I've been a coal miner, a logger, truck driver.

When you were in school did you have any problems with bullying or anything?

Lloyd Caudill: I was one of them that would fight, didn't take much to bullying. I got bullied but I fought back.

Did you ever enter any shooting contests?

Lloyd Caudill: Yes, I have. I've won some and lost some. We'd go and shoot for meat and money. Put up a big pack of pork chops and everybody there would throw a dollar in on it. Everybody would shoot, and whoever shot the best shot won the pack of pork chops for a dollar. Sometimes it'd be pickled eggs, sometimes it'd be pickled boloney.

Did you all have a lot of livestock?

Lloyd Caudill: We had hogs, chickens, beeves, ducks, geese, a horse, such stuff as that. Some of them we sold and some of them we ate. I've got four chickens and six hogs now. The chickens provide eggs. Right now my two hens are sitting on eggs to make more chickens. We keep the pigpens cleaned out, and we worm the hogs a couple of times. The boars have to be castrated so you can eat them. I used to do that for the neighbors. They would offer me money and I wouldn't take it, but some of them slipped it in my pocket and usually I got a bucket full of the mountain oysters to take home and fry for supper. That's the hog balls. You skin them and slice them up like little tokens and then roll them in flour and fry them. Tastes like fresh meat. Now I take the hogs to Amish country once a year to have them killed, cut up and cured and smoked. Been taking them for five years, maybe six. Before that, I did it all myself. My grandpa taught me to butcher a hog when I was thirteen year old. We threw some stuff away like the large intestines, but the small intestines we used to keep occasionally to make soap out of. We didn't pickle our pig's feet.

We just cooked them and ate them. We'd eat the heart, and we'd take the fat and render it into lard and have cracklings left over to make crackling bread.

Did you ride the horse?

Lloyd Caudill: Rode the horse and worked the horse. We plowed with it. We pulled the firewood out of the woods with it.

What did you grow?

Lloyd Caudill: We grew corns, beans, potatoes, peas, cabbages, squash, okra, tomatoes, sugarcane. Just everything. If we couldn't grow it, we didn't go to the store to buy it. We ate what we grew. What extra we had we sold. We sold it to our neighbors passing by. I still farm a little bit. Probably about a quarter of an acre. I grow tomatoes, peppers, cabbage, corn, beans, 'taters.

Who brought in all the money when you were living in your house?

Lloyd Caudill: My dad. He was a school teacher. I had him as a teacher in school.

And how was that?

Lloyd Caudill: Wasn't good. If I got in trouble at school, I got in trouble at the house.

Did you ever get into a lot of trouble when you were a teenager, do any really stupid things?

Lloyd Caudill: Oh, yes. I was just as green as any of them. Didn't know any better. Fighting and drinking. I was put in jail. Just a very short time, just a few hours.

Did you ever build anything?

Lloyd Caudill: Yeah. Houses, bridges, ponds, lakes, roads. Built them for coal companies. I've built four or five barns. Sometimes I had help. If I didn't, it took a whole summer. I built a barn for us to put horses in and to store my and your mommy's junk. We had Tennessee Walkers and a Standardbred. I'd ride here on Field's Fork, where I live. I never left the holler.

What do you remember about your ancestors? What kind of legacy do they have?

Lloyd Caudill: As hard workers. The Caudills are Irish, from a little town in Ireland called Perry on the Scottish/Irish border. There's Indian in my blood on both sides too. My grandmother was a Cherokee Indian. She was a mail order bride. My grandfather bought her out of North Carolina. Her name was Pollyanne. There have been many of my relatives in different wars. I had a so-many-great-grandpa, Benjamin Caudill, he had the first rifleman horse soldiers around here. They were men who used rifles instead of smooth bore muskets and they were good shots, like a sniper. Another so-many-great-grandpa was Colonel Benjamin Caudill, who was in the Battle of Leatherwood. I also had another relative that was a bugler for the Union. My grandpa was in World War I, Battle of the Bulge, he was captured in Germany or wherever. I believe it was eighteen months he was a P.O.W.

Did you ever want to join up with the military?

Lloyd Caudill: No, I have disagreements with our government and military.

Would you change anything or do anything over again if you could?

Lloyd Caudill: Probably not.

Photo by Jessica Ebelhar

Photo by Jessica Ebelhar

SELENA TIREY

Selena Tirey

HOW TO IMPERSONATE A BLIND PERSON

Blind people frequently deal with misrepresentations of their disability. This guide is provided to teach you how to equip yourself with the tools of common social stereotypes in order to perform per typical expectations. Please remember: You are a little blind miracle. You are incapable. You don't know how to care for yourself, let alone others. You are an achiever because you magically graduated high school. You are a coddled invalid. You are Helen Keller. You are Daredevil. Impersonating a blind person is dangerous and may cause bodily harm if not performed correctly. Be careful.

1. Get nimble. Listen closely.
2. Blind people shuffle. Make each step ponderous.
3. Whisper loudly as you walk, calling off each step precisely: *18, 19, 20...*
4. Try to trip people or crack their ankles as you swing and tap your cane in front of you.
5. Stumble here and there.
6. Mismatch clothing. Cross socks.
7. Don't forget the sunglasses.
8. Always remember that cars don't care. People have lives and destinations, and they don't include you.
9. Rock back and forth when you're sitting.
10. Knuckle your eyes.
11. Cut into conversations and keep talking when people have left the room.
12. Prove that you can do things. Anything: shopping, cooking, working a job, writing a book. This will leave many in awe. Some people will pray for you, put their hands on your face, call on the good Lord's power to heal this poor blind person, and use their pity as a conduit for the Almighty. Pity will be hard to deal with; put up with it, though. They mean well, for the most part. Kindness, consideration and compassion are rare but welcome things that should be appreciated and encouraged as much as possible: more of that. Less of everything else. There will be frustration; there will be irritation; there will be disgust; there will be fake concern; there will be apathy; there will always be a wall between you and them. Get used to it, but do not give in to the everything else.

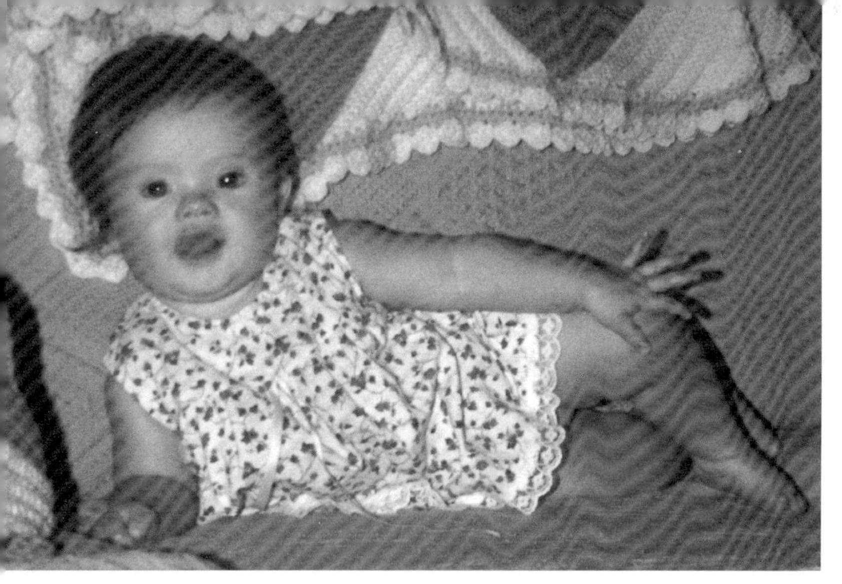

It's a rare and precious thing
to find even a single sighted
memory that's clear.

Photos courtesy of Selena Tirey

Memories are sometimes fickle things. Clear and sharp in some places—a summer sky at noon—and distorted other times. You grasp at them, and they slip between your fingers like fog. The passage of time and the advance of my blindness have dulled what remains of some details, and it's a rare and precious thing to find even a single sighted memory that's clear. I suppose that's why I cling so tightly to the summer days of my youth. Even now, when I hear the old familiar roar of my father's tractor engine, I can feel the world grow just a little bit bigger and I yearn to stand above everything else and see my rural home again, the way I used to.

Sweat drips down my neck, cooled by sudden, frantic gusts that sporadically twist and turn from every side. Rays of light and heat and inevitable sunburn makes me wonder if hell is truly real and if so, did Satan buy some real estate in West Kentucky? Underfoot, dry earth and grass coats my toes, tickling and itching each individual digit. Over my shoulder a roar; a green and yellow behemoth lumbers slowly up and down, row after row, leaving each blade of grass all prim and proper like.

From beneath the shade of our maple tree, I watch my father as he turns down the final row. I scamper out from the shade, hopeful for a single moment high up above the world. His red, sweat-drenched face sees me and breaks into a grin at my antics, waving briskly, before getting back to the work at hand. I can tell by the expression on his face that sweet tea and television are on his mind. The beastly machine growls as Father dismounts and gives me a sweaty hug from which I must pretend to squirm away; we know the drill. "So you wanna help Papa put up the tractor?" Of course I do, and he knows it.

Papa pulls himself up tiredly in his seat, the cushion peeking from beneath the black leather like a yellow spider web. He bends down, thick arm extended toward me, and I can see the green-gray tattoo that wraps around his upper arm, age having turned it into an artistic blur. So many times have I heard the stories about that tattoo. How back in his military days, after he married Mama in the Philippines, he had drawn up a tattoo for both his arms. He lay there for eight hours, snoring while the tattoo artist did his thing. He would laugh and turn to Mama, or shout to the next room, asking if she remembered that day, and bark another laugh at her response. He lifts up his right sleeve and describes with nostalgia each little detail: the eagle, the thorns, the barbwire, and Mama's name.

My tiny hand is swallowed whole by his, and I brace myself against the grooves of the tire, scrambling up like a monkey. There in Papa's arms I feel safe. I have him all to myself and don't have to share him with anyone, not even Mama. My hands strain around the steering wheel. The grumbling motor makes it hard to hear Papa, but I still know what to do. Turning and swerving around the brush pile and trees is as easy as riding a bike.

I watch the world roll slowly past me, Papa's gentle directions in my ear as I circle the brush mountain, dodging jutting limbs. "Alright," he says in his gruff, Southern voice, leaning forward against me, his hands not touching the wheel, but ready in case of any mistakes. "You got it?"

"Uh huh," I say, face scrunched up with focus. I roll slowly passed old Sparky's fenced-in dog yard. The hardheaded spaniel runs alongside, barking and leaping against the fence. I turn past the metal barrels and prepare for the final stretch, spinning the wheel expertly past one of the large trees and praying that I swerved enough to miss those grumpy old roots that always try to catch me. Finally, as I maneuver between two trees, Papa lifts his steel-toed work boot from the pedal and fiddles with the stick shift, lulling the beast to sleep.

The pure, picturesque, details of memories like this one are frustrating little treasures: shimmering reflections of long ago. I could see until I was about fourteen. I'm glad I have memories of sight, when I could see and feel the world more keenly. I can remember sprawling rural landscapes, the field of beans and corn across the road, and the goldenrod that returns every spring. I remember video games that were too hard, and the Christmas tree laden with gaudy ornaments rising from a sea of presents. I understand the concept of color, but now my vision is just a blur of light, moments of darkness that fade in and out, specks of gray flickering like a starry night.

Sometimes I'm taunted by my former vision: when I can't find a simple doorway, when I get left behind in groups, when I deal with sighted people and all their visual cues,

Photo by Selena Tirey

or when I itch to play the latest update to *Minecraft.* I've lost what most would say is a vital part of life and yet, because of that loss, I've made friends, discovered opportunities, self-awareness and independence. Though I sometimes slip into cynicism, I accept my loss for what is, and I try to sift for gold instead of settling for coal.

Sometimes things start out small and snowball. Other times events hit you faster and harder until you can't even feel the impact anymore. There are all sorts of ways for a person to lose their vision. Some ways are sudden: you wake up and some unknown disease has brought you from the vibrant world of color and ease of movement and dumped you uncaringly into the world of blurred shadows or pitch darkness. Maybe it's an accident, a chemical spill, or a vehicle crash that severs your optic nerve or detaches your retinas. There are many ways that a person can lose their vision suddenly, but there are just as many ways for that darkness to creep up on you. I've walked the sighted and the blind path, both. I can say with certainty that neither is easy to tread.

I remember examining the Bugs Bunny cartoons on the frame of my first pair of glasses when I was very small. I asked my Papa why I had to wear them and he said the doctor believed I'd petted a dog and rubbed my eyes, and that now they were a little bad. For most of my life, up until the sudden decline of my vision, that's what I believed. The real cause of my blindness is an extremely rare eye disease known as familial exudative vitreoretinopathy, or FEVR for short. But I grew up not knowing that I had some scary disease. I had fully functional vision and never considered the fact that a person could be blind.

When my math grades started to decline in middle school, I looked back at some tests and quizzes and realized that I'd been overlooking decimal points. We made a couple of visits to my usual eye doctor and a specialist, and they suggested that a good laser surgery would fix my eyes right up and line a few pockets at the same time. The surgeon wanted to remove from both eyes the blood vessels that were causing the issue, but my father drew the line. I remember him saying "Uh—I don't really want to do that." The doctor turned his attention away from blinding me with his fancy miner's lamp and flicked on the lights. My eyes were dilated and I squinted, trying to blink back the lava lamp afterglow.

"Are you sure, Mr. Tirey?" The doctor asked, peeling off his headband and storing it away. "The blood vessels will continue growing in her eyes. If she doesn't get rid of them, she may lose more vision."

"I understand what you're saying, but just do one eye. If she heals up and sees better, then we can do the other eye."

The doctor wasn't particularly happy about my father's plan, but there wasn't anything else he could do. Papa's proved to be the wiser decision because, after the surgery, my vision was even worse. Things that I used to be able to see, like chalkboards and regular-sized print, were impossible to see without using a magnifier. I could still see people, play games, and get around without a cane or another person, but the second domino had already begun to fall, bringing me closer to blindness.

The laser surgery weakened my sight, and when a cocky little kid punched me in the face on the school bus one day the blood vessels in my eye exploded. Our eyes depend on one another, working as a unit. When this balance was upset it became even harder to see, and a blur of brownish red blood floated in my field of vision.

All of this trauma, and the advance of FEVR, caused my other retina to detach itself, leaving me completely blind. One surgery became two, then three, then four; we finally stopped at ten or so. My vision had become so poor that I couldn't walk without clinging nervously to my parents' arms.

Partial retinal detachments, rare eye disease, cataracts, optic nerve severing, corneal blood staining, being short: I had a long list of things wrong with me, and now I had to absorb information in a strictly auditory format. I tried to memorize as much as I could and struggled to comprehend concepts that used to be so easy. I prayed that I wouldn't fall farther behind every day. Learning as a blind person was a rough road, and we had no clue about the technologies and techniques that could make it easier. One day, as my father was researching a machine that could read books to me, the Kentucky School for the Blind popped up on his radar. I remember sitting in a rolly-chair, decked out in my night clothes, listening to my papa read the information from the website. I heard the rubber click of the wheel on Papa's mouse as he scrolled down the page and waited for a report. "Ah, check this out!" he said, startling me. "It says that this place has a summer program."

"What does it say exactly?" I asked suspiciously. Papa read off some information: it was a typical summer camp in the city, tailored for blind kids. You stayed in the dorms, went to some classes that fit the theme of that year's camp, visited a zoo and other touristy places. There'd be a dance to round out the last week. I wasn't all that interested in what kids would be doing at the camp. What I needed to learn was *how they did it.*

In the silence of the office, neither of us spoke. I suppose he held his tongue to allow me to make my own decisions. I was fifteen at the time. Papa told me that I was mature for my age and should have some input in decisions that would affect my life. So he waited as I sat in that office chair, trying to think realistically instead of giving into the fear of the unknown.

"Well?" he asked, turning with a creak in his chair to face me.

"I guess that I should at least give it a shot. I don't particularly like the idea of leaving to stay for two weeks, but I need to see what this place is like."

"I warn you, once I drop you off I can't come back up to get you until the end of the two weeks. I've got to work, and your mother doesn't know Louisville well enough to get you."

"I know...." I sighed, and sipped the watered-down remains of my sweet tea and placed it on the cluttered table. Papa grouched about warping the wood and shoved a coaster into my hand. I sat the Solo cup on the rubber circle. "OK, happy now, you crotchety old man?" I asked with a smart-ass smirk.

I wasn't interested in what kids would be doing at the camp. What I needed to learn was *how they did it.*

Photo courtesy of Selena Tirey

"Yes I am. So, are you sure you want to go?"

"I don't want to. I need to."

"Alright, then." He turned back toward the computer and began clicking. "I'll sign you up."

I went to camp that summer, then enrolled full-time for school in the fall. In September of 2011 my parents drove me to Louisville and dropped me off at the Kentucky School for the Blind. There were no lingering hugs, tearful goodbyes, or excuses to avoid that final farewell before I was left on my own; we aren't the kind of family to get caught up in that kind of sentimental nonsense. Everybody knew why I had to go. That was the situation, and so it shall be. We unpacked my clothes, snugged the sheets tight on my bed, made one last pass to make sure I didn't need anything else, and with a hug and kiss my parents were gone. I left the world of sighties and started my assimilation into blindy culture.

While my mother is from the Philippines, my father and I both grew up and spent our entire lives in one little spot in far West Kentucky. People who aren't from my neck of the woods may claim that folks in Hopkins County are a bunch of rednecks, but that's because they haven't grown up here. The living's slow and most people are kind and helpful. They're as devoted to cigarette breaks as they are to church on Sunday morning, and when you smile at a stranger, they don't assume you're a creep.

Our home is an hour or more away from anything interesting and public transportation is nearly non-existent, but I like living in the countryside amongst nature, though nature doesn't always like me. I'm a country nerd, and I admit to preferring the comforts of comforters, air conditioning, and pillows rather than yellow jackets and dirt. But while I was always playing video games alone at home, I always seemed to make friends with outdoors enthusiasts who were obsessed with horses and tearing up country roads on four-wheelers.

Kaitlyn was one such country girl. Much like any little kids, I guess, we became friends pretty much the moment we met when I started preschool at my old private school. One time, we were driving a four-wheeler around her Nana's farm trying to find an adventure. The tires from the four-wheeler kicked up so much dust that my white hoody became as tan as my skin should've been if I had actually played outside instead of clutching a game controller. I spat into the dirt trying to get the taste of grit out of my mouth as Kaitlyn stopped the four-wheeler. "Check this out," she said, walking into a big reddish brown barn.

Stepping inside that old barn was like stepping into a cave. Shafts of golden light found their way inside, but compared to the bright summer afternoon it was surprisingly dark. "Over here!" my friend called to me as I tried to blink away the glowing dots that wandered in my field of vision. Kaitlyn was standing at the foot of a ladder that led to a hayloft. We hauled ourselves up the wooden ladder and into the loft, where we naturally began throwing hay at one another like wizards casting spells whose magical effect was to make the victim itchy and sneezy.

The giant wooden beams that spanned above the stables and across the open barn looked like the ribs of some giant creature. We thought it would be a challenging quest to race across these splintery ribs to the other side. Neither one of us had enough common sense to realize how painful it would be to fall from that height.

Kaitlyn lay stomach-down on one beam and started half-dragging, half-crawling toward the other side. I tried that at first, but she was pulling ahead of me, so I decided on some drastic measures; I was competitive even back then. I stood up, wobbled until I gained my balance, and began to shuffle across the beam. Shuffling turned into a slow walk that turned into a run over the stalls and their inhabitants. Stabled in the barn was an aggressive beast of a bull whose horns swung back and forth as he tossed his head below me. The exhilaration of running at such a height was intoxicating until one of my small, sneakered feet landed on air and I began to topple off the side of the beam just above the bull. I grabbed for the rib of wood, dug my fingers into its dry surface, and held on with one leg clinging to the rafter. I recall a moment of fear as I dangled there listening to the grunts and snorts of the bull below me, but other than that one instant of frozen time, I don't remember feeling anything other than the urge to not lose. I pulled myself back up the beam, and on hands and knees this time, crawled toward the finish line.

I reached the other side a few feet before Kaitlyn and flopped regally on a bale of hay. Kaitlyn reached me shortly after and stood over me. "Are you OK?"

"Yeah. I'm OK. I won."

I lost contact with Kaitlyn and the others from my old private school, and sometimes I wonder how their lives are and what they're up to now that we're all grown up. Naturally, I check up on them on Facebook, and looking at their profiles makes me feel like an elderly woman seeing little children she used to play with, grown up and living their lives as adults: these little ones have turned into nurses, and saleswomen, college students, and gym aficionados. This one's married off and going on a mission trip to Belize. One old friend has herself a baby and several others have disappeared into the past without a trace. We've all strayed apart, which is, I suppose, natural as children grow into adulthood. We almost never talk except for the occasional happy birthday Facebook message. I'm sure a lot of them would be surprised to find out that I lost my vision, came to Louisville, and am graduating from the Kentucky School for the Blind.

At KSB, I had to play catch up with the other students who all had an understanding of skills that I was utterly lacking: how to use blind assistive technology like screen readers, how to cook, clean, and complete chores, how to read braille, how to use a cane. I had to learn that when you're blind and read with your fingers, you can't eat fried chicken and read braille afterwards. I was just bad at being a blind person, and my ineptitude was painfully obvious to everyone.

In my first few days at the KSB summer program, all the blind kids gathered in a group, waiting for some teacher to tell us where we needed to go. One of the teachers called out our destination, and everyone began filtering out. I hadn't grasped how sucky a blind person I was until that moment when everyone else disappeared outside, seeming to know where to go and how to get there without assistance. I stood there, frozen in panic, not used to walking around in an unfamiliar area without being latched onto my parents' elbow. A teacher walked up and demanded, "Why aren't you leaving?"

"I don't know where to go," I said hesitantly.

"Follow the group, then."

"I can't see where I'm going, though!"

"Most people can't here. It's the school for the blind." She had a good point. I wasn't sure how these blind kids got around without help, and I was too blind myself to realize that they were using a cane.

"Don't you have a cane?" My mind immediately conjured the wooden shepherd's crook that TV blind people used.

"Umm...no, ma'am."

"Well, you need one. Later today, I'll pull you out of class, and give you a cane and some of the basics. We can work on it while you're here."

Another time that summer, we were to make a PowerPoint presentation on the computer. I had no idea how to even sign on to the computer without my sight, let alone make a presentation. I explained this to my teacher, but since it would be some time before I learned how to use a screen reader, or how to work the software, I was left

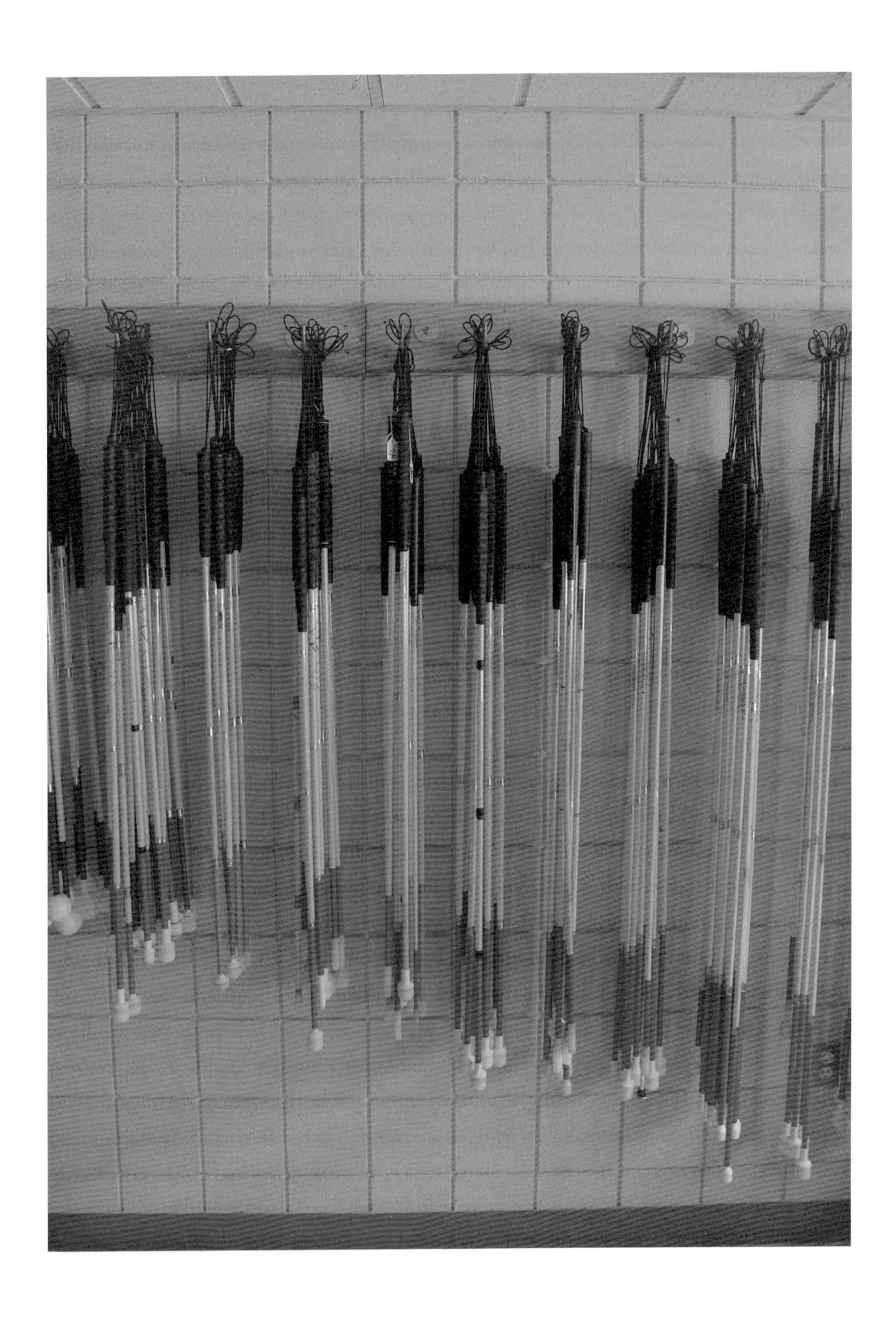

Photo by Kertis Creative

sitting in a chair while another kid essentially did the project for me. I felt completely useless, especially when other kids who were more blind than I was could not only complete the project, but make it all fancy with music and effects.

Back when I was sighted, I used to make all kinds of art on the computer. My father has a passion for digital art, especially the 3D art you see in movies or video games. Papa taught me the basics of 3D programs and paint programs. I wasn't very good at it, but I enjoyed it. When I lost my vision, I could no longer do that form of art, but even worse, I wasn't able to see the incredible art my dad made. I knew that learning how to make a PowerPoint was child's play in comparison to learning a 3D program, which only made me feel my inability even more keenly.

One of the most important and beneficial decisions I have ever made was to participate in the Independent Living Program. It was the reason I came to KSB and a major factor for me staying at KSB when the intrigue and drama of boarding school life got really bad. Sure, I've learned other skills that have helped me with academics or getting around, but being in Independent taught me how to do daily tasks on my own as a functional human.

When sighties cook, they use their vision to keep from burning themselves. When sighties clean, they use their eyes to see what's dirty and scrub it. When sighties go shopping, they just grab a cart, wander the aisles, glance at prices, and grab what they want. When sighties use ATMs, when sighties pay bills, when sighties take money out of their wallet: for anything that sighties do with absent-minded ease, blindies must be taught different methods that work with our blindness and our own personal preference. That's what Independent Program offers.

On Sundays, when all the Independent dorm kids get shipped back to KSB from their home counties, we file in, drop our bags in our apartments, then check in with the supervisors of the Independent Living Program, Chip and Lauren, who have helped me to become a competent blindy. They give us our grades for cleaning the dorm the previous week, and detail new tasks for the coming days. In the Independent Dorm, roommates in each apartment rotate weekly between shopping, cooking and cleaning.

Say I'm cooking one week: Monday, after school, and after my Louisville Story Program workshop, I go back to the dorm and drop off my stuff. Then I and a few others are driven to the grocery store where the newbies shop with Lauren and Chip, while the more advanced students go to the store's customer service desk and request a shopping assistant. Blind shoppers beware: there are different varieties of shopping assistant. There are really great ones who hand you everything, try to get you the best prices, recommend products you may not have tried before, are efficient, generous, patient, and willing to learn how to help blind people. Then there is that one shopping assistant—he who shall not be named—who just assumes what you need, throws things in the cart that may not be what you asked for, and who may or may not tell you when he does this. Keep an ear out for the thunk of products you don't need being thrown carelessly into the cart: we have a budget and can't afford to pay for mystery bag items.

It's around 6:00 by the time we get back to campus, and we still have to carry our groceries to our dorms, put everything away, and fix something quick to eat because we have our Monday meeting with Chip and Lauren. They teach us more independent living skills like how to iron, different ways of paying bills, cooking terms and their definitions, how to properly store food and check for spoilage, cleaning supply safety, and a plethora of other things. Once the meeting adjourns, the chef returns to the dorm, washes dishes and is "free." Keep in mind that I've been up since 5:30 AM.

At night I usually hole up in my room, finish homework, research random things, write fiction stories, and listen to YouTube videos on my phone until I burn up all my data for the month. KSB's proxy and firewalls are set up to deny us any real entertainment while we're stuck in the dorms all week, so we sometimes have to rely on one another. One time, I was sitting at my desk trying to send in some overdue homework. Suddenly, my mind registered something other than the chattering of my computer's screen reader, loud music, and my roommate Kianna's voice. The dorms were renovated a few years back, and we can hear each other through the ceiling and the ventilation ducts sometimes. Matthew and Trint lived above me, and I was frequently concerned by loud bangs, girlish squeals of fright, evil maniacal laughter, etc. This time, it was the most joyous, heartfelt, and out off-key rendition of "God Bless America" I'd ever heard. It sounded like a couple of drunk sailors with too much beer in their bellies and even more free time on their hands. As they hit the chorus again, I guess they heard me doubled over laughing.

"Hi Selena!" Matthew halted his end of the song.

"What are you two doing?!"

Trint finally stopped his howling. "We're singing to people on Xbox Live!"

I just shook my head and went back to working as I called out above me, "Alright then. Don't mind me."

"We can serenade you if you'd like," one of them offered.

"Nah, I'm good. Thanks." The two numb-nuts when back to singing anyway.

There were other things I needed to learn beyond the concrete skills of mobility, technology, cooking, or traditional academics; more obscure ideas that have become foundational to my character itself. When I came to KSB, whether it was simply because we all lived together in dormitories, or because I'd changed somehow, I was able to lower my guard, open up, and be myself. In the process of becoming an adult, I have uncovered some of my flaws as well as my gifts. I've come to terms with my bullheadedness, and my short temper. I've started to understand people more. I've learned that I'm a good listener. I've learned how to be the kind of person that others can go to for help when situations seem to be getting out of hand, how to be subtle went a situation arises that needs a surgeon's delicate touch. I've also learned that I have backbone.

A few years ago my friends and I started playing tabletop role playing games, RPGs for short. The most famous RPG is *Dungeons & Dragons,* but there are plenty more fantasy, sci-fi, and horror games as well. We play a game called *Pathfinder* where you invent characters with special abilities: raging barbarians, healing clerics, magic-born sorcerers, learned wizards, holier-than-thou paladins, tree-hugging druids, rangers, rogues, bards, magi, gunslingers, sexy ninjas, and etc. You make up your character and play your way through a storyline delivered by the Dungeon Master, who runs the game, and is like a story teller who is constantly changing the script depending on what you and your team decide to do.

Even though we were a motley crew of jocks, video game nerds, literature nerds, a theater nerd, a metal-head nerd and anime nerds, some of us were a bit hesitant to make that final leap into nerd-dom that being associated with *Dungeons & Dragons* entails. When I sat down at our table for the first time and listened to the story weaving before me and the dialogue between the veteran players and the Dungeon Master, I began to grasp what this style of gaming could be. Each one of us had our own little scene we had to play through so that we could come together in the plot, but when it was my turn to play my character, to talk like she would, to think of her thoughts and motivations, I froze in my seat, trying to figure out what I was supposed to do.

"Well?" One of the veteran players demanded. "You're supposed to actually talk."

"I know that. She's trying to ignore the weird guy," I lied, trying to cover my mistake. I had to stop thinking of myself as Selena and get into my scene, which involved the Dungeon Master impersonating a creepy dude. I was trying to think of what my character would say to a stranger sitting way too close and staring at her. It's what actors must feel on stage, but my audience was the other players. With a deep breath I accepted the fact that I was about to sound really stupid, turned to face the Dungeon Master and spoke up with a high voice, filled with attitude.

Most people think that I'm obsessed with RPGs because I get to act like a different kind of person with an interesting background and culture, or get to have sexy abilities and look badass. I won't lie. That is completely true and is what makes me an unapologetic

Photo by Selena Tirey

nerd. But that's not the only reason it appeals to me. I know it might sound like a paradox when I say that RPGs help with one's social skills, but I know from experience that they do. Tabletop games disguise life lessons in swords and sorcery, and out of all of these, the most important lessons one can learn, especially if you're going to KSB, is how to work with people whom you may not particularly like. When you play the game, you play a character with their own likes, dislikes, ambitions, fears, ways of speaking, and morality that may or may not be like yours. If you play a character who is shy, gruff, outgoing, cold, mischievous, dishonest, talkative, or whatever, it forces you to put yourself in that character's shoes; it's like practicing empathy.

KSB is a boarding school, essentially, a micro high school. Think about it like this: imagine your own high school, with all of the stereotypical characters present, but condense the population into thirty-five kids, give the majority of them disorders other than blindness, then shove them all into a dorm to live with each other five nights a week for four years, sometimes more. Unlike the drama of regular high school, where at the end of the day you can go home, have Mom do your laundry, eat a snack, and go play Xbox with a couple of neighborhood buddies, we leave the school building with everyone, walk down the ramp, and follow the sidewalk with our canes until it branches left and back to the dormitories. Saturday is, effectively, the only day when we're not constantly surrounded by one another and KSB staff. Even KSB teachers don't seem to fully comprehend the closeness between us students. When one family member is angry, we're all angry. When one thing happens to upset the blind flow, the effects ripple out to touch all. We are individuals, but we are also an entity, and when something happens on the blind grapevine, we are all affected. KSB claims we're all one big, happy family. Deep down, we know it's more accurate to say "dysfunctional family" than anything else: still family, though.

Sitting at a table with friends, following the twists and turns of plot and feeling the camaraderie that only slaying a hoard of orcs, killing the Storm Queen, or discovering the traitor in our midst can provide, broadened our imaginations and gave us something in common to get excited about. For a few hours we found respite from the stresses of the upcoming week. It gave us some time when we weren't blind kids with personal issues that plagued us, but adventurers with pressing dilemmas and ambitions. When I play my characters, I can't be put aside so easily. If the mission is to be a success we need each individual member's abilities. I'm part of a team, and the unspoken camaraderie says no matter how much we dislike one another we will stand together and win this.

I've persevered through a few battles in my life. I made it through the surgeries, dealt with the loss of my vision, graduated from high school, completed the Governor's School for the Arts, and am going to be a published author: I learned how to impersonate a blind person, and then I learned how to *be* one. Now I'm thinking about my life as an adult. I want to pursue a degree in the human services field so that I can help people in need change their lives for the better. No one's ever truly ready for what the real world has in store; life is full of what *Dungeons & Dragons* calls "random encounters" which crop up when you least expect them. During those battles it helps to have an ally by your side, somebody who's already defeated a goblin or two.

Photo courtesy of Selena Tirey

First snow

ANGELITA ESTANDARTE TIREY

My mother is from the southern islands of the Philippines. When she was a child, she and her siblings split their time between attending the village school, and working for food and money to support the family. Like most young adults there, she moved to the capital of the Philippines, Manila, in hopes of finding more job opportunities. My father was in the military and stationed nearby. They crossed paths and were later married on the day that Papa was to board his ship and leave the country. Eventually, Mother emigrated to the United States to our home in West Kentucky. She is a certified nursing assistant.

I was born in 1965 near Surigao City, Philippines. It was just a small community. It didn't have a lot of people. But when I went back in 2002, it was overcrowded. I didn't even know the people down there anymore. A long time ago, from the house where I grew up to the ocean was a long walk to us, but when I went home last, the place was all houses and houses and houses, like it's getting closer and closer to the ocean.

My mom is Dolores Estandarte and my father is Lucratio Estandarte. My father drove a jeepney, which is a long, open passenger car that doesn't have any seat belts. My mom had a little bitty store, and sometimes she'd go and get some fish from people who knew how to fish, and then go to a different town to sell the fish.

I have three sisters and three brothers: Fernando, Danny, Ramil, Jossie, Alona, and Rosalinda. I'm the second oldest. I was little when my mom died from complications from the birth of my youngest brother, so my grandmother is the one who raised us. We had no electricity. We usually didn't have any running water at home. There was only one place that everybody in the whole community had to go to get our drinking water and wash our clothes.

When I lived there, when we went to the well to get our water, we would have to go past this empty area. Because there weren't any people there and there weren't any lights, we were kind of scared, especially at night. When we'd go home, we ran because we were afraid there might be some ghosts or aswangs. That's what we were scared of. There's a story to that. It's an old wives' tale, we really don't know if it's true or not. They say that when a woman's pregnant, if you lay flat on your stomach, then aswangs will get your baby and sip the blood of the baby or something. I heard about aswangs since I was little. If you heard, "Tock tock tock tock tock," you know, crickets? We'd think it was aswangs. Woodpecker? We'd think it was aswangs. Everything you heard from outside was aswangs. Especially at night.

My grandmother was a *hilot*, a healer. When anybody needed to be massaged or had fever or any stomach ache or anything, my grandmother would do herbs. She knew which herbs to give to make people get better. That's why she was popular. They didn't pay her. Sometimes they would give her some rice or a can of salmon, and we accepted it because we needed food. Sometimes they'd give us some sugar for our coffee.

My grandmother was really struggling to raise us, so we had to pitch in. She fixed fishing nets when they had holes in them. It's like knitting. She'd find somebody with a fishing boat so she can make money. We planted crops so we could sell them, or we'd go fishing. We'd go to the ocean and get some fish and then we'd sell it.

Sometimes we had to be absent from school to plant rice, because if we didn't, we weren't going to eat. Planting rice is hard. Especially because I'm scared of leeches. When you plant rice, it's really, really muddy, and that mud's got a lot of leeches. I had to keep an eye on my legs. When I found some, I screamed and my grandmother had to get them. We didn't have any choice, because that was the only thing we could do to eat. Sometimes we didn't have any food, and we had to struggle to find something. If we didn't have any rice, we ate root crops. Everybody pitched in, looking for food. We planted rice so we could eat, but it takes a while before you can harvest it, so you have to find a way to find food in the meantime.

Even when we were little, ten or eleven years old, we'd have to wake up at 4:00 AM to cook and clean the house. We'd have to leave at 6:00 to go to school. They would usually give us an hour lunch, so at noon, we'd come home and cook and eat, then go back to school again around 1:00. At 5:00, we'd go home, we'd cook, and then before we'd eat we'd have time to play outside with the other kids in the road.

We didn't have any yards, so everybody had to play in the road. We used to hit this tin can with our flip flops, or we used a stick. Sometimes we had jump rope. You didn't have to have expensive stuff. We just found anything we can think of. It was just a regular life. Just being poor. I guess that's why I buy shoes and purses now: because I couldn't buy them before.

The holidays I remember were Christmas, New Year's, and Fiesta. Our fiesta in Apayao is on June 24. Our patron saint is John the Baptist, Señor San Juan, so we celebrate that for a week. We do a procession, bring a saint and all those idols to the ocean, and we ride in a boat from place to place.

We didn't have any presents on Christmas. Everyone went house to house caroling, and they had fireworks. Especially in Manila, and especially with New Year's, everybody had fireworks.

Four of us have moved out of the Philippines: me and your Aunt Josie and your Aunt Rose and your Aunt Alona. My brothers are still there. We send money so they can have something for New Year's, because for New Year's you need money. The tradition is that you have to have all these round things in your house; you need a lot of food that is round, like apples, or oranges, or whatever.

I grew up a Catholic. We went to church Monday and Wednesday and Sunday. Sunday is the big mass. It's like here: they have singing, they have communion, they have a choir. When I was little and when I was in high school, I was part of a choir. And we had another little group they called "Legion of Mary."

During my first year of high school, I worked for people who sent me to school. By our standards, they were rich because they had a piggery, they had a rice field, they had land, and they had a nice house. They put me through school, but I had to work for it. I had to wake up early to feed the pigs, and then help cook for the people. Then my grandmother's cousin, who had money, sent me to school. I went to her house as a maid.

I went to Manila when I graduated high school. Everybody goes to Manila. I worked everywhere. I worked in a sewing factory, a factory making wheels for luggage, another sewing factory, and a peanut butter factory, and I worked as a maid. No matter where you go, it's always hard work, but you have to do it.

I didn't stick in one factory. Kept moving. Every time a cousin told me, "There's a good job there," I took a different job. You just work and go home and work and go home. If you're a maid, just work, work, work. If I worked in the factory, me and my cousin just rode a bus or jeepney and go to our destination, worked, came back again, and went home, that's it. It was boring. I lived at the factory one time because they only paid 150 pesos for fifteen days, 300 pesos a month. Food was free, but you still had to send money home. You still had to buy your own stuff, like shampoo, lotion. You had to find cheap clothes or shoes so you could have new stuff.

Sometimes there were Americans in our town and we would be amazed. We looked at them like they were really important. We hadn't even heard about Americans before. Your daddy was walking with a little boy as his guide; he liked to sight-see. My friends were hanging around in the road, you know how it is when there's nothing to do. I saw him coming, and I told my friends, "He's going to be my husband." I was just kidding. He didn't even hear me. He was far ahead. Then my friend introduced me to him, and I guess he liked me.

Photo courtesy of Selena Tirey

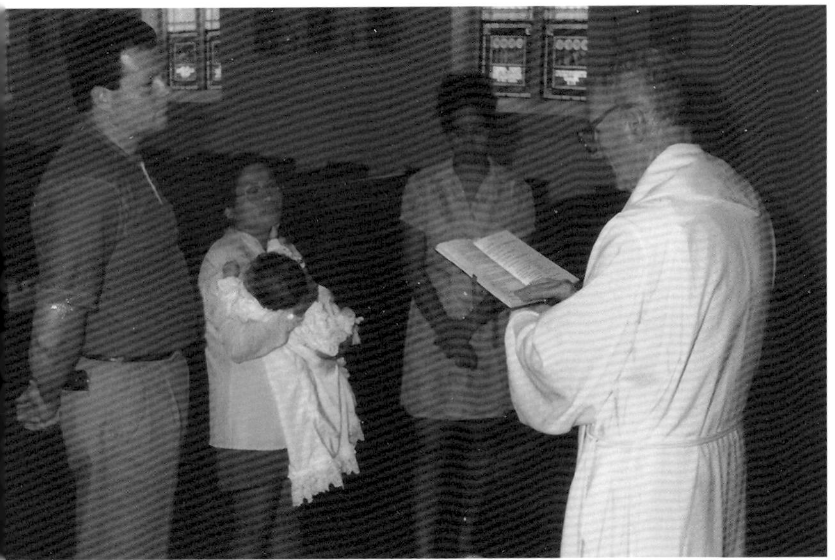

Photos courtesy of Selena Tirey

That night when I met him, he was supposed to leave; their ship was going to Manila Bay. I said, "I'm supposed to go home to Manila tomorrow," and he said, "Don't go home yet." That's where it started. He came back two weeks later and we became fiancés. After that, the paperwork we needed before we could get married took a year because he was in Japan. The day the paperwork was approved, we took it to the priest, and then we got married in a church around 6:00 PM.

There was a big typhoon and raining, a big storm. We were not prepared, but we really had to get married because he was going back to Japan at midnight that night. After our wedding, we went to a restaurant while it was pouring and storming. After a few hours, he went back to the ship and back to Japan for six months. It was just a really fast wedding, and then he had to leave. No honeymoon. "Goodbye."

Even though I was married into the military, under the US government, it was a year before I could come here because of the paperwork. It's not easy.

Your daddy sent me money when I was still in the Philippines and I had a good life there. My grandmother didn't want to ride the ships, didn't want to ride an airplane, and I couldn't go back and forth. The only thing I regret is that I didn't get her a better life like I got. I sent money, but I wish she could sleep in a nice bed. Because she struggled for us. She was our rock. When she passed away, I couldn't get home. My passport was not done. But I don't have any regrets. I love your daddy. That's why I'm here.

When I stepped off the plane in America, I was skinny and little. Daddy had gotten me a pink coat. Auntie Nancy wanted me to bring a Philippine doll, and I couldn't put it in my suitcase because I don't want to get it wrinkled, so I had to carry it with me. I must have looked like a little kid. When I landed there was snow. It was the first time I'd seen snow: white, really white.

Photo by Jessica Ebelhar

Photo by Jessica Ebelhar

HALEY HALL

Haley Hall

SOMEONE OUT THERE HAS YOUR BACK

When I was fourteen years old, I left my family and my friends in Breckenridge County to learn the skills I need to be independent someday. Five days a week, the Kentucky School for the Blind is my home. I have friends here and some amazing teachers who care about my well-being and my success. At KSB, I'm learning to make the best of things, to advocate for myself so I can get what I need and want in life. Living in Louisville is easier for a blind person than living in Hardinsburg. There are talking crosswalk signals here, and identification domes in the sidewalk let a blind person know they're at a crosswalk when they hit them with their cane tips. Transportation's easy. Whether it be buses or taxi services, there's always someone out there able to help you get around. I like how sighted people in Louisville have learned to adapt to the needs of individuals besides themselves. But when I look out the window here in Louisville, I don't see all the trees I used to see at home.

My real home is in the country, in the middle of nowhere, in Breckenridge County, Kentucky. Even for rural America, Hardinsburg is a small town; we have five fast food restaurants and the third smallest Walmart on the planet. But Breckinridge County is a beautiful place. We have so much peace and quiet there, and I couldn't ask for a better home community. Everywhere you look, there are cows and beautiful horses and lots of people who are always outside. I love going back in the woods to see all the different trees growing there together and all of the colors that are mixed together with all of the wildlife roaming the woods. Barely any cars ever go by. After dark, when the responsibilities of living on a farm are wrapped up, all the kids come outside to play with their friends. I love to run barefoot in the backyard and to play hide and seek, staying outside as long as I can, running out back to that big open pond in the neighbor's yard and fishing, and camping for the weekend.

I love my home, and I miss it, but I know I can't live in Breckinridge County: there's no public transportation and it just isn't accessible to the blind or visually impaired. In Breckinridge County it's hard to find a job if you don't live right in town or know how to farm and raise livestock.

My grandad, Thomas Wayne Hall, Sr., was a farmer. He raised nine kids, had fourteen grandkids and one great grandchild. He believed that people need to do things for themselves and always told me that my mommy couldn't hold onto my hand forever. So even though I couldn't see the best, he expected me to be out there on the farm helping out as much as the other kids. Grandad always wanted all of us involved in the activities that occurred on his farm. We watched as he would give a calf its shots or fight a cow into the trailer. We helped in the garden planting beans, radishes, and peppers, plowing, pulling weeds, depending on what part of the season it was. We could never help too much. "The more the better," he would always say.

Grandad was the type of guy who didn't like to be stuck inside. He was outdoors whenever he could be. When it rained, he'd stand at the door looking outside, just sighing every once and awhile like a little kid. He had hazel eyes, and a little bit of light grey, almost white hair. Once I complained that somebody had pulled my hair and he said, "Well, you could be like me and have no hair," rubbing his bald head. He was hard of hearing and not very talkative. I spent more time at Grandma and Grandad's house than I did at home growing up, and Grandad practically raised me. He had the kindest heart I have ever known, but he did like to tease his grandchildren. It absolutely tickled him pink whenever one of us got upset. My grandma, Juanita, would sit back and laugh watching him tease us like he did. I could tell they loved each other, though they never showed it while they were in public.

When we would drop by the farm for a visit, Grandad would always be waiting for me with the tractor running so we could take a ride through the woods and go to see the fields and his cows. We'd get on that tractor and I would smile at my daddy as he opened the gate for us, and giggle with Grandad all the way back through the woods. There was one tree I always looked for on that path; Grandad told me it was the tree my daddy played on when he was a little boy, and I always jumped off the tractor to play on it too until the day that the tree fell apart. All of us grandkids played on it like our mothers and fathers had before us, but years of weathering had gotten to it. It stormed really badly one night, and when we went to play on the tree the next day it had fallen down.

Past the barn was the chicken house, and the chickens were my job. I fetched the eggs and brought them to Grandad while he distracted them with chicken feed to keep them from pecking me. After that was done, I put those eggs in my shirt as we drove back up to the house. Daddy would be standing there waiting for us to come back so he could open the gate. He would always say, "Did you have fun?" Dinner was usually ready by the time Grandad and I got back up to the house and washed our hands. Grandma Juanita is a country cook who loves making spaghetti and Hamburger Helper, or what she calls goulosh. When you are in the Hall household you either eat or it will be gone, and there will not be more for a while. Grandma doesn't prefer a table cloth unless we are celebrating a big occasion. She takes the food out of the hot pans and puts them into plastic bowls on pot holders. As we ate our dinner, Grandad would tease us or tell us stories. He always reminded my brother, sister and me not to ever get too close to the farm equipment by showing us the scar on his arm. Whenever Grandad was younger, he got his arm caught in a combine while helping shuck corn, and it hung like that for almost thirty minutes. He would tell us how much it hurt but how he never cried about it.

Photo by Haley Hall

One day just before dinner, we were sitting at the table. I looked out the window by the kitchen sink and saw dark clouds covering the fields just as lightning flashed. Grandad knew I was terrified of thunderstorms. Once it started to thunder, I did what I always do and started whimpering. To get me to calm down Grandad started assuring me that the noise I heard wasn't thunder, that it was just the dogs, Tigger, Tess, and Coco, rolling around on the porch. He stood up and went to the door, and acted like he was yelling at the dogs, telling them to stop rolling around. I argued with Grandad until dinner time about how it was not the dogs we heard, that they were laying on the porch, not rolling around.

On March 24, 2015, my grandfather died of a heart attack doing what he loved to do: taking care of farm animals and farming land that he had owned for years. Whenever I get upset, I ball all of my emotions up inside until I finally and break down and cry. But sometimes, music can calm me down. After Grandad died, I was listening to my iPod and heard the song "Lean on Me." When the chorus came on, it brought up memories from the past with Grandad and other family members, like on different holidays whenever we would meet together at Grandma and Grandad's house. We would all have a party and celebrate seeing each other, showing that we all cared about one another and would be there no matter what happened to anyone in the family. Knowing that Grandad would want me to be strong, I decided I would listen to the song a few times and try to calm down a little more.

At Grandad's funeral, so many other people were upset about losing him too. I tried to help them feel better and see that Grandad would want them to be happy and not cry over him being gone. I'm grateful "Lean on Me" was written. Everyone struggles, but you don't always have to depend only on yourself; sometimes someone out there has your back and won't let you fall. It's good to be reminded that when someone needs a friend to lean on they can get what they need. I miss my grandfather like crazy, but I know that he is watching over me.

Photo by Haley Hall

He was tired of people making fun of him, so he got the surgery when he was fifteen. It lasted seventeen hours and he died a month later.

Photo courtesy of Haley Hall

I am the only blind one in the family, but my sister Brooklyn, my mother, an uncle, an aunt, and I all have a hereditary disease called Crouzon syndrome which causes the premature fusion of the skull bones and affects the shape of the head and face. Most people end up with shallow eye sockets, and as a result, their eyeballs appear to protrude or bulge forward. Because Crouzon affects many different areas of the skull, surgeries to relieve the pressure on the eyeball orbits, the jaw bone, and the cheek bones are performed in stages at specifically recommended ages. The first surgery is a craniectomy. The second procedure crushes the bones in the eye sockets and pulls the forehead forward. Next they pull the cheek bones and the jaw bones forward, and on and on.

As I got older, my eyes started to turn outwards from the pressure and my vision got worse. I would have to get extremely close to see anything, and my teachers told my parents they were worried about my sight. Everyone knew that I had Crouzon, but the specialists in Owensboro told my parents that I would grow into it, and that I didn't need surgery. Not everyone with Crouzon gets the surgeries. For instance, my sister and my aunt Christy never had them.

Momma thinks that the doctors waited too long to perform the surgeries to release the pressure on my eyes. The recommended age for the first surgery is between birth and nine months old; I went into the hospital at five. The surgery was only two hours, but I was in the hospital for two weeks, and rested at home for another month.

When I was nine and they told Mom that I needed to do the second surgery, the one on my eye socket, she asked me if I wanted to continue with the surgeries. For a long time I'd heard the adults talk about my mom's uncle Cricket who had Crouzon too. He was tired of people making fun of him, so he got the surgery when he was fifteen. It lasted seventeen hours and he died a month later. When Mom asked me if I wanted to keep getting the surgeries every couple of years, I thought of Cricket and said no. But I was talked into it after all. After four reconstructive surgeries on my head and face, I'd had enough, and I never got any more. My vision never got better.

I remember waking up in recovery the first time and not being able to open my eyes more than just a crack because they were so swollen. I could hear everybody around me, but I couldn't open my eyes to look at them. My daddy and my momma sat on either side of me, rubbing a cold wash cloth on my forehead. Once I opened my eyes, I noticed my cousin Tyler in the corner. I heard my uncle say, "Its OK. It's just Haley," and I looked over in time to see Tyler hide behind his daddy, crying and shaking in fear, scared to death of me. He was too young to understand what was happening, but it was upsetting to me.

Someone had brought me balloons, the kind that have a picture on the front and a shiny back. I pulled them down to me and used them like a mirror: in the shiny light of the balloon, I looked like an alien lying there. The bald area where my hair used to be frightened me; I loved my hair, and now it was gone. My eyes were so swollen. I felt and looked like someone had hit me in the face and blacked my eyes. It wasn't pretty. Somebody noticed that I was crying and moved the balloons.

I can look at you with both my eyes, but my left eye is totally out of focus. It drifts and bounces, moves on its own, and I can't see anything with it. Once, when I asked my second grade teacher for help with something, she looked at me and said, "What are you looking at? Your eyes are going in every direction. Why don't you look straight?" This really hurt me, and I made it a point to be crying when I got home that day. I told Momma and Daddy about what had happened. Dad wasn't very happy to see me crying. He knew that this teacher had given me similar problems before, and it was the final straw for him.

My daddy is a big man, about 6'4", and strong. He grew up on Grandma and Grandad's farm and has done his share of hard work: wrestling cows down to give them shots or slaughtering them for beef, baling hay, driving the tractor with the hot sun beating down on his back. He has brown hair, hazel eyes and a hot temper, especially when his kids are unhappy. You can tell when Daddy is mad because he starts breathing heavily out of his nose. I do the same thing when I get upset.

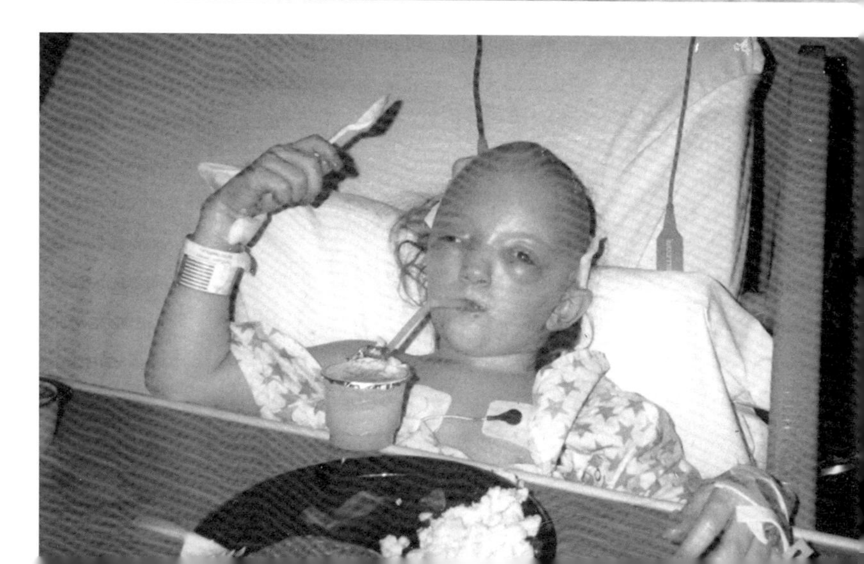

Photos courtesy of Haley Hall

When I told them what happened, Momma tried to calm Daddy down, but there is no stopping Daddy when he is mad. He went out to the car and quickly left the driveway. While Daddy was gone, Mom sat and had a talk with me. My mother looks a lot like me. She doesn't have Crouzon syndrome as bad as I do, but her eyes bulge out a little more than mine; she knows what it's like to be picked on, knows what it's like when people don't understand and jump to conclusions. "Things will get better. I promise," she said.

Mom knew I needed more help than I was getting in Breckenridge County Public Schools. She wants me to have more than she had growing up. She wasn't able to go to college and get the career that she wanted, and she raised three kids on very little money. Mom could see my struggles with me getting bullied and would always tell me how kids are cruel that I just needed to keep my head held high and keep pushing through the bullies and the people who didn't understand. My mother has always told me, "Do what you want to do and never let anything stand in your way. You are a strong, beautiful little girl." I couldn't ask for a more helpful family. I love them to death.

Daddy pulled back into the driveway and got out of the car. He'd gone up to my school and demanded to talk to my teacher. The school wouldn't call her to the front desk, so Daddy had left her a very strongly worded message. He wouldn't tell me what the note said. He wanted to keep the problem between the adults, and only told me, "I took care of it, Haley, and it won't happen again." When I got to where I was smiling and laughing later, Daddy seemed satisfied to know that he'd fixed my problems with my teacher.

When I got to school that next morning, my teacher acted a lot differently. She treated me like one of her favorite students. It was like someone had opened her eyes to see what it was like to walk in my shoes for a while. She started treating me more like a student who could do things, and less like a person who needed her hand held for everything. The rest of the year was enjoyable for me because she made me feel like I was important in the classroom.

By the time I went to middle school, my vision had gotten worse, though not as bad as it is now. My vision teacher only came to see me twice every three months, so I didn't get much in the way of special instruction. I was always asking the teacher for help. I struggled a lot. I fell down the steps a couple times a week. I had to have someone else do my computer work for me because it hurt my eyes so much. Finally I advocated for myself, spoke up about the struggles I was having, and they bought me a great big magnifier with a terrible glare that I had to carry around with me everywhere; believe me, I tried to break that thing every chance I got. I started using a cane that year too. Carrying around a giant red and white stick didn't help me fit in much.

The bullying was the worst of all. I got bullied every day. I was one of the sweetest girls in school, but everyone called me "gross." No one wanted to be anywhere near me. People told me I was stupid because I was blind and had to get really close to the classroom doors to see the numbers, and because I had to ask everybody what to do and where to go. When they bumped up against me in the hall they'd say something like, "Ew, I touched it!" It hurt, and I went home crying all the time. I fought my instinct to retaliate, and I tried to let it all slide off my back. My mother always says I have to be the more mature one. It's mature to be able to follow the Golden Rule and treat others the way that you want to be treated.

One day in sixth grade, just as I was thinking how lucky it was that my regular bullies hadn't met up with me yet, they found me at my locker and pushed the books out of my hands. "See, guys? She is clumsy," Trey, the leader of the group, said. I knew better than to bend down with him standing there. Trey had sent me to the nurse before with a bloody lip. He'd been picking on me since we were younger. Whenever he had the chance, he'd find a way to hurt me, whether it was kicking me in the face or shoving me onto the concrete or into a chain link fence. He pushed me up against my locker and laughed just as a couple of my friends walked past and caught the terrified look in my eyes.

"Trey, why are you doing this again? What did Haley do to you?" my best friend Cody said as he pushed his way into the group, grabbed my hand, and led me away from them.

"Cody, why don't you mind your own business." Trey pushed Cody against the locker and swung at him, but one of Trey's buddies grabbed his arm as a teacher came through and broke up the circle. Trey looked back at me. I couldn't stand to let him see my face, so I ducked down to pick up my things.

Later that day at lunch, Cody and a few of my other friends sat down and looked at me uncomfortably. I knew what was coming. They were going to tell me that I needed to start standing up for myself, that they wouldn't always be there to stick up for me. I'd had this talk with my friends multiple times. I always tried to straighten up and be the stronger person but that never seemed to work. I am the type of kid who will hide over in the corner to keep away from trouble. I never wanted to get myself involved with all the crap bullies wanted of me. But even when I tried to stay out of their way, they usually just tried harder to find me and hurt me: the more I hid, the worse it was for me. My friends in middle school didn't understand the stuff that I have to go through. Nobody knew how to fix anything. I took what people think about me too seriously. People talked about me, and my self-esteem was so, so low. It was torturous.

I finally got fed up with up it and stood up for myself. There was usually a group of kids who'd follow behind me when I was walking around the football field on the track. Around the corner where nobody could see us, they pushed me down and I scraped my knee. I was frustrated. When I got up they started talking about my eyes, and my anger got the better of me. I knocked one of them on the ground and walked away. When you treat a bully the way they treat you, they tend to back off; they didn't mess with me again that day.

My mom knew how hard a time I was having, and she did some research on the Kentucky School for the Blind and found out about the summer camp program. One night, as I struggled to do my homework, she was talking to my daddy to see if he thought it was a good idea. I listened in on their conversation and found out that I was going to the camp whether I wanted to or not. My momma sat in the living room and when my daddy came in from working on his old truck, she had the application in her hand. "I tried talking to her. She said she doesn't want to go to this camp." Mom tried to whisper so I wouldn't hear her. Daddy didn't care. He just spoke normally. "Well,

Photo courtesy of Haley Hall

this is going to help her more than her school will. I am sick of seeing her struggle." The next day they sent in the application for the camp.

In 2012, I came to the summer camp at KSB. Honestly, I wasn't too interested in the camp, but it got me away from my parents for a while. I didn't know anyone, so I was scared. I stayed for maybe a day before calling my mother and father to come and get me. My dad wouldn't let me come home; he wanted me to be able to show that I was a big girl and didn't need my mommy and daddy everywhere I went. After I got off of the phone, I noticed that none of the girls at camp were anywhere near me. They were all hiding from me. The next day, I tried to talk to people and nobody would talk to me because I was new. After lunch, I called my momma. "Momma, I want to come home. I don't like it here." I wasn't crying yet, but I was close. Momma could hear the sadness in my voice and told me it would all be OK, I just needed to try to stay up there. "But Momma, no one will talk to me and they are hiding from me." By this time I was in tears. Sure enough, I got my way; before she hung up she said, "I'll be there in about an hour or so. I love you. Try to have fun." When we got back to the dorms, the girls started to talk to me and I started to have fun. I wanted to tell Momma never mind, but I decided that she was coming to get me and that was that.

Camp was better the second year, and the reason I decided to move to KSB for school is because I met my boyfriend, Justin. We were both shy people and didn't want to talk to each other to begin with. Sitting at the lunch table one day, Kianna introduced us. We both raised our heads, said "Hi," and put our heads back down. That Thursday at the farewell dance, we were pushed into each other by our friends and told we should dance together. I liked how he was so sweet to me, and he was also really cute, so I swapped numbers with him. That summer I didn't plan on moving to KSB, but he helped me decide that the Kentucky School for the Blind was better for me then my public high school.

A few months before I went back to summer camp and then moved in at KSB for high school, I had a day I wish I could forget. I was pretty happy as I waited for my ride home from school one day, and then I was picked up by my grandmother. Now, normally, a little girl would be happy to see her grandmother, but when I got in the car I had a bad feeling in my stomach. Nauseated, like you would feel if you had just eaten some bad food and your stomach wants it out. What was happening? Why was I having this feeling?

When I asked Grandma Sue what was going on, I didn't know that the answer to my question would be the worst thing I'd ever heard. She told me that we were headed to the courthouse to sign some papers so she could become our legal guardian, and that my mother and father had gone to jail earlier that day. I immediately started crying. I didn't want to live with Grandma and Papaw. I was mad at the world. It was like the world was standing back laughing at me and my pain of not being with my parents. At Grandma's house, I watched as it got dark outside, and it sunk in that I wasn't going home. I was stuck. I was a momma's girl, always holding her hand and standing right next to her. I wasn't ready to live somewhere else. I just wanted to go back to my home and live happily like before. I cried the whole time.

I never really cried when I was little because I was not allowed to do very much. My parents were what you'd call hover parents. Since I was about three years old, when I started to lose my sight, I couldn't fall down without my mother running over to me saying, "Oh my! Are you OK?" and picking me up off of the ground. If I just sat down a little too loudly, she was at my side. After my first and second surgeries, when I saw double for about a month, I wasn't allowed to find my own way anywhere. When I wanted to get out of my bed I had to call for my daddy to come and carry me where I wanted to go to.

One day I was hungry and nobody was coming when I called for them, so I found my way to the kitchen by myself, walked into a hot stove, and burned my hand. I got yelled at because they were worried about me, and said that I should have gotten one of them to help me. They wrapped my hand up so it would heal. I remember being so annoyed with them at the time, but now as I look back, I am glad that they cared enough for me to try and protect me.

I am very independent, and I don't want my mommy guiding me everywhere I go in life. But that first night at Grandma's, as it was getting dark out, I wanted to go home to my family. I wasn't feeling well. I felt sick to my stomach. Grandma asked me to do some simple thing like clean the dishes, and I snapped at her. She sent me to my room where I lay face first on my pillow, crying to myself. It was so hard to accept that my parents weren't coming back, that I was staying with my grandmother in her house and wouldn't be going home for a while. I thought about how she was just like Momma, yelling at me whenever I got attitude. But then I thought about all the things that Grandma was doing for us: if it wasn't for her, Brooklyn, Thomas and I would all be separated. I made the decision that I needed to straighten up and show that I was thankful.

Grandma's house is a little bit stricter than the home I was used to. Grandma and Papaw are old-fashioned, and I didn't like that at first. When I'm not at KSB, I have been living with them for almost three years now, and I've learned to like living with them. They have taught me the importance of growing up and doing things for myself like saving money and advocating for myself when I need help with just about anything. At my grandmother's house, I'm expected to try and take care of myself. Grandma makes me help with cooking whenever I am home with her. Sure, she is afraid that something bad could happen, but she wants me to learn.

I love my momma and know she is only trying to do what is best for me. She misses us kids. She says the court is going to let us all go home again soon, but honestly, I don't know if I want to go home anymore. We all look up to her and always hope for the best, but being separated from your hero doesn't help children much.

The night before I moved to Louisville to attend KSB for my freshman year of high school, I lay in bed thinking, "Are you sure you want to leave the school with all of your friends? Do you want to leave Breckinridge County and your home community, and move to the city?" I had myself second guessing even though I already had friends here and was already accepted into the school. As anyone would do when they are having things like this going through their head, I made a pros and cons list.

CONS

1. I'm leaving my hometown where I grew up, where I have all these friends.
2. I have to make all new friends and it's hard enough for me to talk to people as it is.
3. I don't like the fact that I'll be living at my school.
4. I know I will miss my little sister Brooklyn and my brother Thomas.

PROS

1. I want to succeed in life, and KSB can help me do that.
2. The teachers there can help me more.
3. It's right next door to the American Printing House for the Blind. There are resources.
4. My boyfriend Justin is there.

All of it gave me a headache and I didn't want to think about it anymore, but I knew that the Kentucky School for the Blind was my best bet. There was so much opportunity for me to succeed and do the things I wanted to do. My public school was holding me back. Sure, I'd cry on the last day of school, but it really helped me to hear my friends say, "Haley, don't cry. We understand why you want to go, and we support you." We still keep in contact (whenever I am not grounded, that is), and I send emails back and forth with some of my old teachers.

When I got to KSB I made some new friends and experienced the actual life of how it is to be blind. I realized that there are people who can relate to how I was treated in public school and who can understand me, people who know how it feels to be in a sighted world with little or no help. I can be free here. The teachers actually care and show us how to be successful in a sighted community, how to not end up homeless, living in a box somewhere.

The last three years have been quite an experience for me. I have done a lot of growing up. I have learned that things are not always handed to us and we eventually have to work on our own. Going to visit my parents in places where I couldn't even give them a hug, leaving the comforts of home to move to the Kentucky School for the Blind, making new friends: it's been hard sometimes. But I've stayed at KSB because it is the best place to help me succeed in life.

I have more self-esteem now. My boyfriend Justin and my best friend Kianna have taught me that a real friend will be right there by my side no matter what, and that I can't let people walk all over me and make me feel like crap. In the past, my kind-hearted nature sometimes held me held back; well, not anymore. When people laugh at me for using a cane, I just hold my head up a little higher and walk on.

Photo courtesy of Haley Hall

Wide steps. Strong heartbeats.

ALISA HALL

My momma's name is Alisa Marie Hall. She is 36 years old and just wants the best for her three kids. She wants us to have more than she had growing up. I love my momma, and I know she loves me too.

Life for me growing up? As a child, it was grand. Thinking about it now, there was a lot of fouled up stuff that I didn't realize, but as a child it was great. We had no real connection to the outside world, no house phone. All me and my brother Michael had was each other, I guess. We were always at home. We would play hide-and-seek in the cornfields. We used to footrace a lot and ride our bikes a lot. When we'd start our races, we'd always sing, "One for your money, two for your show, three to get ready," and it's supposed to be "four to go," but he'd always come up with something else. When we'd get about halfway across the yard, he'd start clapping his hands. We played down in the edges of the woods in the creek. Thinking about it now, it was just a dump hole, but in our minds it was, I don't now, like a horror story. We were like investigators, digging up evidence.

Michael and I used to have very creative ideas. One time I convinced him he could fly; he jumped off a building with a towel tied around his neck. Of course he splatted. He was upset about it, and I told him he was doing it wrong, that he had to have a trash bag. So he got back on top of the building and jumped and still couldn't fly, and this time he hurt himself. Mom started squaloring, so I just jumped too. That way he couldn't get me in trouble for telling him he could fly off the building.

My parents were my superheroes, but they weren't around a whole lot. My mom worked all the time, and Dad was gone. Dad used to be an alcoholic. When I was younger there were a lot of fights, but when things were going good and they were on the same level, like when we'd go to the zoo or something like that, it was great.

Michael and I were like night and day in school. He was always getting in trouble, and I was always not; I guess it's vice versa now. I always enjoyed school, other than the bullies, of course. I always tried to put my best effort into my work, but the bullies made me doubt myself or made me look away or not want to succeed.

I had glasses back then. I mean dorky glasses, the tinted ones, you know what I mean? I'm sitting in class one time, and I know something's not right. I notice all the kids are laughing, but I was used to them laughing. My teacher said, "Alisa," and had me come up to her desk. She said, "Let me see your glasses, honey," and she got tickled. One of the lenses had popped out, and here I'm wearing these glasses with one tinted lens and one not, and I can't figure out what's going on because I'm so focused on the bullies, and my feelings getting hurt, that I don't realize my glasses were busted. So she got the lens and fixed my glasses for me.

My favorite hobby was basketball. I was really good, and I didn't realize it. It started because Michael wanted to play Saturday morning basketball, and I was more or less there just to watch. I wasn't even interested in basketball, but my talent was recognized, and after that I made the fifth-grade team and the sixth-grade all-stars. I mean I had some mad skill. I've kept my awards, my certificates, stuff like that. I was so proud of them, maybe because Mom and Dad never came to my ball games. Maybe it was just wishful thinking that they would one day be recognized. That's why I try to talk to you all and tell you your good deeds. Did I have anybody preaching that or teaching me that growing up? No, I learned it myself.

Being a grown up sucks. It really does. I said the same thing you do, "I can't wait till I'm out of school," and now I regret it. I wish I had focused on what needed to be focused on instead of just trying to get by. Even with the biggest heart and the strongest head, the real world is hard. Because life is nothing but continuous tests. You've got to make life what you want it to be, and that's why I keep pushing you all, so you won't struggle and have those continuous tests. I regret not pushing myself to my true potential. I regret going above and beyond for all the wrong people. All the Lord asks of us is to be ourselves, and it's kinda hard when you gotta be what everybody else expects. It sucks not being able to just be yourself.

I really didn't have a normal teenage life. I had to grow up faster than I wanted to. So I didn't have time to focus on that. I've always been a worker. I was always out in the tobacco fields from as long as I can remember. I had to start working. I was babysitting my little sister Caitlin, too. She's fifteen years younger than me. One time your dad and I were trying to keep Caitlin distracted, so we found her a rope and a stick for a fishing pole. I told your dad to make it look more realistic, make it look like she was going fishing. So we had a paper clip for a hook, and we got her fishing. I said, "What are we gonna do if she catches a fish?" He said, "She ain't gonna catch no damn fish." Well, ten minutes later Caitlin grinned ear to ear. "Look, guys, I got a fish." It was so priceless. You should have seen the smile on that baby's face.

I have a lot of memories with Caitlin. One time, I was getting ready to clean my bedroom, to take the laundry to the laundry room. Any other time I'd let her sit there because I had one of one of those great big round mirrors on one of those old-timey dressers, and she would just sit and play. But this time I was like, "Come with me and help me put these clothes in the washer," and she went and helped me. No sooner did we get the washer loaded than it sounded like a bomb went off. I froze, and Caitlin about jumped out of her skin. I was like, "What the heck?" First thing I did was run outside, but there was nothing outside.

I walked back in the house and looked around the living room and the kitchen and I thought, "I have no clue." I opened my bedroom door and it was full of smoke. The ceiling had fallen through. And that old dresser had broken clear in half. Could you imagine what it'd have done to her if she'd still been standing in there? Any other time she would've been in there playing, jumping on my bed. I won't ever in my life know why I asked her to come with me that day, but I did.

Photo courtesy of Haley Hall

I was nervous when I found out I was pregnant the first time. I'd been getting sick at school, and I had this feeling, a suspicion. I went and got my pregnancy test and went to the bathroom. When the test said positive, my motherly instinct already kicked in, because I knew it'd be all right. Later, I went to the cemetery and sat there where Uncle Cricket and all of them are buried. I sat and talked to him. I was scared. I was nervous. I was everything: all emotions mixed in one. I had all my emotions running through me, even the ones they don't even have a name for.

I didn't really have any needs or wants or any worries until you were two years old. When I saw you struggling with your sight, it tore me up inside. It hurt, and I wanted to take it away from you or understand it, but I couldn't. I was frustrated, thinking there could've been something done, or it could've been prevented. That hurt, because I didn't know. You'd like to think that all mothers hurt when their child's hurting, but there's a lot of parents out there who don't care.

Have I ever got to a point where I struggle? Yes. Have I ever got to a point where I'm discouraged? Of course, but to just give up altogether, no. If I ever got to that point, I'd whisper your names and my heartbeat would get stronger, my step would get wider. I kept pushing. You all are what makes me want to keep going every day. It's the same thing that has kept me going for the last seventeen years: Haley, Thomas, Brooklyn, Haley, Thomas, Brooklyn. You are my heart and my world. Without you all and your daddy, I wouldn't have my smiles. I wouldn't have my anger. I wouldn't have my craziness. I'd be just a normal person. I'm not normal by far, and that's why I push for you all to not be normal. Be the fearless one that goes a separate way. It's gonna take a lot of heart and a lot of insight to be able to endure the taunting that may come with it, but I promise you, if you can step up enough to go that separate way, you'll be better off. I can't find anywhere where it says life is fair. But it is a blessing, a gift from the Lord. It's taken a lot of heart to pass my tests, and a lot of help from my family and friends and most of all from Jesus. It's a lifetime of hide and seek, of finding him—the Lord—and yourself.

Photo by Joe Manning

Photo by Jessica Ebelhar

SHANE LOWE

SHANE THE SHEEP IS ONLINE

The bus was one of those older ones, made in the '90s, I guess. You can tell because the seats are smaller, as the buses themselves tend to be. I remember it smelling horrible, like someone had dropped a few spoiled eggs in the back and left them to torture the next hapless blind guy who merely wanted to ride home in peace. I was on my way home from a long, stressful day of the fifth grade, and I just wanted to sit down and relax. It was a miserable trip, but I made it to my grandparents' house with minimal illness, and stepped off the bus into suburban Pleasure Ridge Park. Cars flew past me to the left as I walked toward the house, the afternoon sun beating down relentlessly on my shoulders.

Even though I had my cane with me like always, I didn't need it to navigate the path to my grandparents' house. I knew the distances by heart, could hear the sounds around me, and wound back and forth in a series of steps leading up to their front door: *ascend driveway, beware low-hanging branches of tree to the right, step up to sidewalk, slight turn right, up one more, short sidewalk straight ahead, four steps to front porch, avoid maiming*. Inside, I couldn't tell the difference between the air-conditioned foyer of my grandparents' home and the entrance to heaven.

In the kitchen, I sat in one of the rolling chairs at the table and opened up my laptop. I'd had it since 2009, and the casing was worn where my hands had rested for so long. It was old, battered, and had seen too much use. My grandmother sat down nearby and resumed her game of *World of Warcraft*, and I started logging into a website where some of my blind friends hung out and played games.

I engaged my screen reader, a program essentially used to assist blind people with getting around computers. It recognizes and announces everything on the screen in a synthesized voice of the user's choice. The voice I use is called Eloquence. Whether I'm playing a text-based game, chatting with someone, reading, or editing audio, Eloquence is constantly babbling relevant information in my ear, often for hours on end: I do a ton of reading. If I put my mind to it, I can sometimes knock out 300 to 500 pages in a day. When a sighted person hears Eloquence's absurdly quick, synthesized speech, they rarely understand a word it's saying. I grew up with a screen reader speaking everything to me, though. It's what I know. That's how I've used computers all my life. Eventually, that speech got too slow, and I realized it would be more efficient if I increased the speed. Currently, I read at about 850 words per minute with Eloquence; normal conversational speech is something like 150 words per minute.

The site I visited was one where blind people from all across the world go to play games together: Monopoly, Uno, Blackjack, and others. I joined a game of Uno with a fellow whose username was Hady. We started playing, and amid the constant sound of flipping cards and my grandmother humming to herself in the background, we wrote back and forth to each other. I told him about school here in the United States, and he told me about Egypt, where he lived as a blind person with his wife. We started talking about Skype, which was still sort of uncharted territory for blind people at that time, and how I wanted to set up an account because some friends were trying it out. Because it was a relatively new tool for the blind community, we didn't have an easy way to install it. I told him of my problem, and without hesitation, he agreed to help me. I was amazed.

Most of the people I spoke to at the time weren't very polite to me. The middle school I attended at the time was full of haters and bullies. Hell, I don't fit in at the public high school I attend for part of every school day now. For starters, both schools are predominantly African American, but never mind that I am paler than an anemic vampire: I'm blind, and that comes with a whole different set of stereotypes. I'm never Shane at school. I am "The Blind One," or, occasionally, "The Funny Blind One."

Outside of classes, I never kept in contact with anyone from my public school. I had no one's address, no one's phone number. I barely knew anyone's name. Few people talked to the blind one, so I wasn't used to the type of instant kindness I was getting from an Egyptian man on the internet who I hardly knew. He set up my account for me in no time, and I was overjoyed. I logged in, and it was actually working! That night, I added several friends as Skype contacts, and many of us then decided to use it in place of the phone for our discussions.

Compared to how many friends I have in public school, I feel like the Kanye West of the internet. I could run for president! I have actual friends there. I am never thought of as the blind one, not even the funny blind one. On the internet, I'm Shane: I'm known by my actual name, not a physical trait. My personality is appreciated and, when I work on things like the internet radio station that my friends and I have, it feels like I'm a part of something. The conversations are amazing, and friendships feel truer; we aren't friends because of clothing or popularity, circumstance or geography. That kind of thing doesn't matter in the immaterial world of the internet. It's all words and personality there, and that is why I believe so many blind people make homes there. Some think that people online are all fake friends, or 40+ year old kidnappers who want to eat children's souls, but I've made a lot of real friends who I hope will be around for the rest of my life.

I owe a lot to that Egyptian guy. Every long-distance laugh, every conversation that leads to another big change in my life, it's all because of his kindness, and his willingness to help me, a stranger. I have met people I hope will be lifelong friends, and I met most of them because he was generous enough to create that account for someone who couldn't do it on their own. We have since fallen out of contact, and to this day, I regret not asking him for his name, I suppose it just slipped my mind. I do remember his old Skype name, though:

You.Will.Stay.The.Best.

Every long-distance laugh, every conversation that leads to another big change in my life, it's all because of his kindness, and his willingness to help me, a stranger.

Photo by Jessica Ebelhar

Many would find it strange that I can communicate on the internet so freely, while elsewhere I am very self-conscious. The reason that I'm nervous in person is because people can see me and, as such, they know things about me that I don't even know about myself. I don't know what people *look like*. If you haven't been blind since birth it's hard to understand this, but I want you to think about it: I don't know what a face looks like, so I don't know what faces *do*. I've never seen a single wink, shrug, or smile. All I've ever seen is brightness and darkness. I understand the essence of black and white only by their absence in each other.

Everyone smiles when something makes them happy or is funny. I'm no different—I'm great at smiling—but I don't know what smiles *look like*. Neither do I know what it looks like to be sad, angry, or worried. I have a lot of trouble forcing a smile for pictures or anything else if I'm not actually feeling happiness or amusement. I'm not sure how to recreate what I do naturally. The same applies to things as simple as walking, holding a fork correctly, or which way I'm facing when I speak with someone: I never know if I'm making some tiny error that's so obvious to the rest of the world, but that I can hardly comprehend.

I perceive the world through my ears. Most everything that happens makes a sound of some sort, and I use those sounds to find things. It's called echolocation. If I click my tongue against the roof of my mouth, the soundwaves from the click travel around the room and bounce off of all manner of objects. I can hear walls, cars, people, trees, and pretty much anything else that is at the level of my ear when the sound bounces back to me. I am, essentially, a giant wingless bat, and I'm not ashamed of my unsettling nature!

Even though I can't see how someone looks, I can hear expressions in the tone of their voice. It's what any sighted person tries to do when they're on a phone call, but we blind people do it constantly, and we're good at it. Barely concealed undertones can describe what a person really thinks of you. I can tell when someone is faking an emotion. I can hear a smile in someone's voice, and the same goes if they're worried or sad. True happiness is very difficult to fake. I pay attention because I always hope to make the people I love happy. Whether that be helping a friend or family member through a tough time, or spending a day out with my girlfriend, Madelyn, every moment of those experiences is important to me. I want them to know I'm there for them, and that I can be counted on to help.

I sat at the bar in our kitchen, hearing the soft sound of the television somewhere in the background. The kitchen opens up into the dining room with the fancy table for when we host family events, but my brother Hunter and I usually eat at the bar, Mom and Dad in the living room, and someone will occasionally eat in their room if they're busy or feeling antisocial. The counter wraps around to the kitchen's far wall and the door to our pantry. Its formerly impressive contents had been whittled down to the bare essentials, and those only remained because Mom had stocked up to compensate for our manly cravings.

My little brother Hunter came in then, his camouflage hat proudly on his head, and his eyes shielded by new glasses that had one end on a string running around the back of his head to the other which I like to tease him about. He sat in the vacant seat next to me and started surfing YouTube on his iPad. Dad sat on the couch in the living room behind us. We could hear him talking to Mom on the phone through the doorway. "She's pulling in the driveway now," he said to us. "Alright," I replied. Hunter removed his headphones, and reluctantly tucked them away.

The garage door opened, and Mom walked through, her heels clacking on the tile floor and bags rustling in her arms. She placed several items on the dining room table, and walked around the counter to face Hunter and me. She dropped something else onto the bar, but it didn't sound like a grocery bag, or her purse. "I brought KFC," she said. Usually on Christmas Eve, she or Dad would cook something, or we'd go out to a fancy restaurant with someone in the family. I understood why she'd gotten carry-out, though. My parents had been stressed a little recently. Mom had just gotten a new job, and something had come up with Dad's, making it possible that he could get laid off soon. We were worried, and Mom hadn't had the energy to cook some nights. Hunter didn't mind; I wonder if he even noticed. I understood, and tried to help where I could.

Dad walked into the kitchen, and sat down at the table. I moved to join him, but Mom placed a plate in front of me before I could get up. She dropped a chicken leg onto my plate, followed by a scoop of mashed potatoes, another of corn, a third of coleslaw, and a biscuit. I didn't know how I would finish it all. Mom served Dad and Hunter, then sat down and started talking to Dad about his day. I listened quietly, eating without thought. Even though I was feeling particularly antisocial this Christmas Eve, we stayed in the kitchen after dinner to talk a bit. At that time in my life, I found it difficult to talk to my family about most anything. I felt bad because I knew they were worried about me, but it's like there was a presence in my throat sometimes, fighting down every word I wanted to say, pushing it back into mental penitentiary.

I appreciated the opportunity to hang out and talk, though I likely didn't show it very well. It wasn't that I resisted socializing, I just didn't smile or seem particularly energetic. Talk turned to Christmas Day and the party at our grandparents' house. We spoke a little about presents, and what us young folk did that day. Then Mom turned to us, gently placing her glass down in front of her. "So," she asked. "Do you guys remember any nice Christmas dinners we've had before?" Something about this question, its simplicity, and sentimentality, just crushed me.

All of us were quiet for a while, and I imagine my face went through a series of expressions: first the look people get when they are thinking, going far back into their mind to remember the most infinitesimal details. Then I likely looked happy for a moment. And finally, sadness because of all the times I did remember but couldn't say out loud. I don't know why. I just felt like I couldn't say them. Yes, Mom, I do remember. Last year, when our grandparents came over. We got really comfortable pajamas that night, and you made honey-glazed ham, and a new kind of green beans that we always eat now because they were so good. 2012, when we went to "Jerry's" with your side of the family. We started the tradition of getting Christmas pajamas that year, and I was grounded that day. Dad had taken my laptop away, and when we were about to go back

There was a presence in my throat sometimes, fighting down every word I wanted to say, pushing it back into mental penitentiary.

Photos courtesy of the Lowe family

to our rooms, he went into the garage, threw some wrapping paper around it, and gave my computer back to me as an extra present. And the year before that, when Dad made grilled chicken and the round fries that were my favorites when I was younger, and still love today. I do remember, guys. I remember. Vividly.

It was such a simple question, one that we could have talked about in a heartbeat. I'm sure the others had to remember something too, but they all stayed quiet like me. Thinking back on it, I wish I'd had the courage to share those memories with my family; I still regret not talking about them. My chest still tightens thinking about how I could have made everyone happier, if even just for a moment in that brightly-lit kitchen. Finally, Dad turned to us. "I remember this one time when we got KFC," he said. Mom and Hunter chuckled, and I forced myself to laugh with them.

I couldn't stay much longer after that. I excused myself and walked back to my room, where I took my place in front of my desk. It's not a very fancy desk, battered and cluttered, but it's mine. I do have a system evident enough to anyone who truly cares: CDs stacked on the far left, external hard drives next to those, ready to be plugged in. Behind the externals is a small mess of cables, another external, and a pocket knife for the packages I'm too weak or lazy to open with my bare hands (likely the former). My laptop is set up in front a pair of speakers, and to the right of it are several thumb drives, my microphone for professional use, and a couple of tasty winter green mints. To the right of my desk is a file cabinet, which is pressed back into the far corner of my room. A random stack of paper and my Braille Sense—a device many blind people use like a tablet with a built-in braille display—sit on my old piano stool.

I signed back into my computer, quickly scrolled through the few Twitter notifications I recieved through the internet radio station I worked with, then engaged my broadcasting software. I had a radio show to do that night: a Christmas-themed radio show entitled "Santa's Twirkshop." I hoped it would take my mind off of the real world for a while.

If you think about it, a song, a paragraph of text, or a softly spoken word can give someone a completely new outlook, like flipping a switch. I like to offer that to others, so I am a writer, I host an internet radio show, and I'm a good friend. But, if I could be remembered for anything, it would be the music I play. There is very rarely—I'd venture to say never—a day when I don't wish to play, talk about, or listen to music. It's something everyone can understand, a universal language.

When I need energy, rock and heavy metal are always there. When I'm unhappy or depressed, there is always acoustic rock, or simply softer songs that will bring out clarity for me. If it's been a particularly bad day, and I need to sleep, I'll listen to piano music. I also love orchestral music, which helps me get into different moods when I am writing. When I play intense games on my laptop, or am setting up a show, for example, I play intense action-themed orchestral music in the background, and when I am in a somber conversation with someone, slow, sad songs generally come from my speakers.

I love rock music. It brings everything together. The pounding drums, powerful vocals, and shredding guitars always get me hyped and improve my mood. Since I was very young, I've listened to classic rock with my father, bands like The Scorpions, Def Leppard, AC/DC, Bon Jovi, and Mötley Crüe. I remember riding in the car when "Who Says You Can't Go Home" by Bon Jovi first came on the radio. My parents insisted it was really Bon Jovi, but comparing its country sound to some of the band's harder rock from the late 80s, my six-year-old self refused to believe it was the actual band; rather, the DJ had simply made a mistake, and no harm done.

When Mom got into hip hop like Nelly and Lil Wayne, it became my obsession too. Every day, I'd spend an hour and a half on the bus going to and from school listening to artists like Tech N9ne, Meek Mill, and B.o.B, comparing who could rap faster or freestyle better with my friends. My mainstream rap stage lasted quite a while, but I was too poor to buy music when I was eleven, so I found a YouTube video-to-MP3 converter and manually downloaded Eminem's entire discography song-by-song.

Shane Lowe

Photo courtesy of the Lowe family

As one could infer by my music obsession, I love going to concerts. There's something about live music that gives people energy. Sometimes, for a brief moment, your problems go away when you're swept up in the raw emotion as the same songs that form the soundtrack of your life are being played live in front of you. I have hated the studio version of a rock song, only to fall in love with it when I heard it live.

When I was a kid, the biggest venue in Louisville was Freedom Hall. Despite its seating capacity of around 17,000 people, it wasn't big enough for the popular rappers of the time. But I went to classic rock shows with my father occasionally. I saw AC/DC with him in 2009 on their Black Ice tour, and Heart with Def Leppard on their Mirror Ball tour in 2011. Both of these shows were fantastic, but nothing got to me remotely as much as the Bon Jovi show I saw in 2013. That's when my love for concerts really began, and now I see shows live and on the internet all the time.

There are people who record concerts and sell them, but a true music fan would never sell an artist's music for profit. The hundreds of thousands of people who share concerts online for free do it because they love and appreciate live music and their favorite bands. Whenever I am too busy or can't afford to meet up with my friends at a show, there's a good chance we can all get together online and have a good time listening to a concert for free.

I can't remember when I first heard a song or a DJ babbling on the radio. The idea of talking to so many people in so many different places at once has always astounded me, though, and I was very curious to know how it worked. One morning when I was pretty small, maybe first grade, I decided I wanted to put together my own radio setup. I went through the French doors to the master bedroom in my grandparents' house where my grandmother had a fancy corner desk that made a nice little place for me to chill. I took a tape deck, a CD player/FM radio, and the landline next to Grammy's computer, and decided I was going to start being a DJ. I called my friends on the phone, put it on speaker, and played music and talked to them like we were hosting a real radio show. I recorded everything we said on the tape deck, and I think I still have some of those cassettes. These early DJ experiments inspired my creative side; I knew I had to get into radio, and after hearing my first internet radio station, I knew I could. When most people think of radio, they imagine top 40 mainstream songs played over and over again with a peppy announcer talking about contests, concert tickets, and endless advertisements for things like car dealerships and gentlemen's clubs. That's not what I was interested in, though. I wanted a place where I could speak to the world about what I love, and show it off.

I indirectly discovered internet radio when I was ten years old. I had just joined an email list for blind people interested in computers and other spectacularly nerdy topics when I stumbled across a website out of the United Kingdom. I started browsing around the site and came across a podcast series about technology accessible to blind people. Another section of the site was devoted to what were called audio games—games based entirely on sound—and after playing a few I was hooked.

I had been playing my way through a particularly difficult action game, and I found an audio review of it on an internet radio station. When I clicked on the review, the host didn't just play the game, but had co-hosts who phoned in on Skype and bantered about other irrelevant and hilarious topics. It immediately grabbed my attention, and I knew I had to call in.

DJ D answered on the second ring. I lowered my voice a bit, trying to remember some of our biggest vocabulary words from English as I did my best to introduce myself as if I did this kind of thing every day. In the midst of proudly informing the listeners that I was thirteen (I was ten at the time), my father came into my room. Later, I would come to understand the importance of the mute button on my phone, but in that moment, I could only sit by in terror as he said, loud enough for the entire internet to hear, "Shane, it's time to brush your teeth." I made the split-second tactical decision that it would be best for my image to hang up without speaking, and that's precisely what I did. Despite my shame, after I brushed my teeth, I decided to call back. I spoke much more quietly this time because I was supposed to be in bed, but it was still an amazing experience! That was the first time I was able to have my own voice broadcast to the world, and it felt great. I was hooked, and I wanted to be a full-time co-host, maybe even have my own show one day.

When I was thirteen for real, I kicked off a show called The Arcade in which I and several friends around the world sit down for anywhere between two and six hours to do what we love. The show usually begins with one of my trademark introductions featuring a heavy metal or orchestral soundtrack and immersive sound effects to get everyone ready for a long night of amusement. I open with a set of three to five songs, from artists like Ed Sheeran and Halestorm, to a Vince Neil cover of an Elton John song or part of the *Legend of Zelda* game score. From this point on, every aspect of the show aside from the technical production is controlled by listeners, and anything goes. Listeners can chime in through social media or by voice chatting with us live. Discussions range from politics to unfortunate incidents in the shower, from music requests to ideas for games we should play, and books we should talk about. There is a brief period of contained chaos known as "The Library," where we discuss what we're reading at the time, usually fantasy novels, and more specifically Brandon Sanderson and Brent Weeks. All we aim to do is entertain, and I hope that every now and then, our formula of action and anarchy makes someone's day.

I used to be stuck in a sort of bubble. I am, in general, a shy person, and tend not to do very well with first impressions. Going to a school like Central High, where most everyone seems so drastically different from me, can be very off-putting and make it difficult to find true friends. When I was younger, I'd play with some of the neighbors on our street, once even trying to play a little "B-ball" with some of the teenagers that lived three houses to the right of my back door. As I got older, though, I realized that I didn't have much in common with people who played sports in the driveway, jockeying for who got to ask the head cheerleader to prom and who must ask the girls lower on the pyramid. Sometimes I'd chill with my younger brother and his friends, but our

Photo courtesy of the Lowe family

interests started to differ as well. My friends at the Kentucky School for the Blind all lived in the dormitories, and I wanted to spend more time with them, but I couldn't because my family is in Louisville and I lived at home.

So, with all of the people physically near me drawing away or unavailable, I turned toward my trusty laptop for entertainment and companionship. Over the last couple of years, I have found a group of people who share my interests. I spend hours every weekend speaking to friends on Skype and on my radio show discussing what we've all been reading lately, authors we like, and what we hope to see come out in the next few months. We spend hours singing along to some of our favorite artists as if we were really with them and 75,000 fans in a stadium in a different hemisphere. (Fun fact: my singing voice causes 80% of the untimely demise of small creatures living near me.) I don't know what I would do without times like these, times when I and my friends are all swept up in what we love, when we can forget everything else.

It would then come as no surprise to know that I met one of my best friends on the internet. Her name is Precious, and I've never actually been in the same state as her, let alone the same room. I don't think it makes a difference that we've never occupied the same space, though. Despite not going to parties together, or going out for dinner, we have always gotten along. We have talked for hours at a time, and often watch concerts together or listen to new music that we find interesting. We both enjoy the best fantasy authors, and are very musical people. In fact, she has started a full double major in music education and vocal performance at the Berklee College of Music in Boston, where she grew up with her Puerto Rican family.

Precious is an epic procrastinator, but still gets things done and has time for those she cares about. There's just something about her, a sort of openness, I guess. She is the kind of person who lets nothing stand in her way, and makes what she believes in happen despite what anyone else thinks. For instance, her first solo album, *Hummingbird,* is coming out this autumn. I try to be like her, dedicated, and determined. I also try to emulate her open-mindedness. If someone offers an explanation of something, Precious always considers what they're saying, their justifications behind an action. She weighs and considers everything fairly. We have helped each other overcome many obstacles, and no matter what happens or stands in our way, we know that the other is always going to help as soon as they can. It's amazing to know nothing will happen to this friendship any time soon.

I have attended the Kentucky School for the Blind for about ten years, and have split my time at public schools as well. Unlike some of my classmates, I don't have a glorious and heroic story about coming to KSB. I was born blind and was used to special classes to help me learn things like braille. My visual impairment has always been more of a regularity rather than a disability. I started at KSB how most people did: at summer camp. Dad worked downtown, and mentioned one day that he drove past the school for the blind a lot. He found that they had a "nifty" summer camp for visually impaired people around the state to meet up, and I gave it a shot when I was very young, around five years old. I enjoyed the camp, and a year later my parents and I decided that KSB was a better idea than public school. The biggest reason I asked to switch was the rumor that I'd have to take a state test in first grade at the public school, and I was not having that. Also, I had zero friends in public school, and had managed to make some at KSB summer camp.

Even so, by the time we were all in middle school, I began to understand how drama starts and plays out: X tells Y their problems, Y informs Z, and so on. Arguments and pointless anger over a trivial issue stressed everyone out for no real reason. Because of this, I never really spoke about my personal life with anyone. I became withdrawn from most of my peers and spent most of my time speaking to friends on the internet and playing games. I still had some who I called friends, but I wouldn't tell them about anything that was bothering me because I was afraid of drama and judgment. I was a fair-weather friend in reverse. But after my freshman year of high school, I was an emotional wreck. I figured it was time for me to let someone get close, someone who wasn't on the other side of the globe.

Although I've known Madelyn since the glory days of KSB summer camp after kindergarten, I never had meaningful experiences with her until one summer before my sixth grade year. I ended up leaving camp early that year because I was tired of dealing with the faculty and needed more time to myself. At home, sitting in my room one Saturday evening after I'd left, I was thinking about how frustrated I was. Long story short: the year before, I had asked a certain chica to the infamous KSB summer camp dance. She denied my friend, but lo and behold, when I asked, she agreed. We danced during one song, and in my young mind it was our happily ever after. But during this year's summer camp, she'd hardly spoken to me. It hurt. I felt like I was a joke, and her friends were laughing about me behind my back. I was through with that, and as KSB's deity of immature entertainment, I decided to do something.

That night, I called up my homeboy J and together we used Skype's phone call feature to give a ring to this fine lady who'd wasted my precious time. J was a master of audio disguises and could make his voice sound drastically different with ease. Prank calling is an art: there are a series of delicate steps, the first of which is to be ready to throw your plans out the window and improv like Amy Poehler on steroids if needed. We had that in the bag. "Hello?" she asked. As J began speaking, I wrote him a quick instant message as to how he should proceed. "Hello ma'am. This is the Louisville Metro Police Department and we've received reports of harassing calls being made from this number to one Shane Lowe. Would you know anything about that?" The seriousness in his tone almost had me convinced that a cop was monitoring the call, and had stepped in to run the prank for us. She told us she didn't understand what was going on. That Shane was just some annoying kid from last year. I could hear her voice rising, fighting the panicked belief that this could be real. As the call continued, she started to get hysterical, and we played off her reactions to get new material to work with. She broke down in tears at one point, and despite my childish glee, I was starting to feel bad for her. That's when she gave the phone to Madelyn. "I don't know who this is, but there's no harassment coming from this number. I know the person who owns this phone a lot better than you do, so don't think you can just call and assume things." As soon as I heard her voice, I knew we were playing a completely different game. J froze for a split second, and in the silent lingo of prank calls, we knew we were done. His serious act was slipping the next time he spoke, and with me only able to play the distraught, nervous, and very harassed Shane Lowe, I couldn't do much to hold up our story. She saw through it from at least the second sentence. I admired her unwavering self-confidence, and wanted to know her better.

Madelyn is confident, determined, and doesn't take a lot of BS. She could tell you sixteen ways you're wrong about something, but she'll turn around and defend you to an outsider because she's loyal. I admire Madelyn, and fell in love with her because of her personality, the way she thinks, and the way she communicates. Sometimes she's serious, but I'm jokey and relaxed. She wants things to be a certain way and executed precisely, and I'm more chill. I just see what happens. We balance each other out. She's also beautiful.

Sighted people think that blind folk go around feeling everybody's faces, which is crazy and kind of hysterical. Sometimes I'll joke around and tell someone, "Yeah I was just out yesterday, met a couple new people and felt up their faces." It's a joke because it's really weird to just feel up somebody's face. We don't do that. I don't even know what my family physically looks like. But when we're more intimately close to someone, we will touch their face—much as a sighted person would—and through that we know what they look like. Looks don't matter to us, but through that we learn something new about the person. The first thing a sighted person knows about someone is what they physically look like. For a blind person it's the reverse. It's the last thing. The last step. It's hard to put into words what Madelyn looks like. I know that she has a perfect face, though.

Four years after my prank call, a very different phone conversation occurred, again with Maddy on the line. We were both at our homes for the weekend, and it was somewhere after one in the morning. I'd just finished listening to an epic Bon Jovi concert on my laptop, while she had just finished a musical. I was exhausted, and staggered toward my bed. Maddy said, "I love you; sleep well," and I fell asleep,

Photo courtesy of the Lowe family

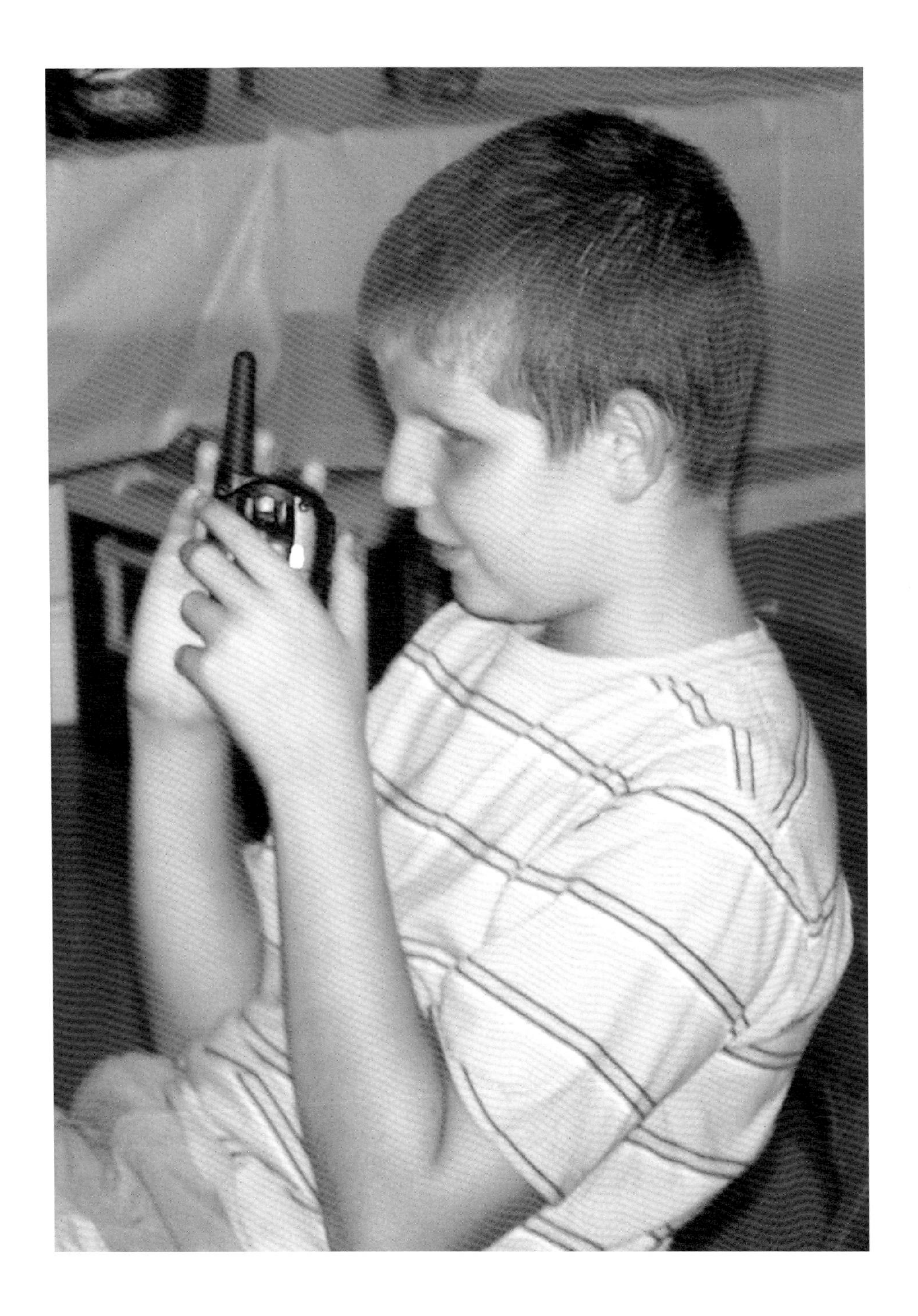

Photos courtesy of Madelyn Loyd

for hours I guess. When I woke up, my arm was dangling over the side of the bed, and my phone was still on. I put it back up to my ear, and heard Maddy talking to her sister, some intense murmuring, then a gasp, then what I could swear was the word "pregnant."

Plot twist: Madelyn and I had a baby! Kayson Oliver Lowe was induced on May 24, 2016. I'm a dad now. If you don't believe me, there are endless pictures and videos to prove it. Let's be real: having a baby is terrifying regardless of how old you are. I can't imagine not being a bit nervous when you find out that you've just started growing a little creature, and that very same mystical being is yours for the rest of your life. But, even though it was a lot to take in, we never considered adoption. If this is how the cards were meant to fall, the best advice I had for myself was to stack the chips, neatly, and play the game.

Kayson's actual birthday was very busy. We got to the hospital early. Madelyn was induced at five in the morning, but Kayson wasn't born for another thirteen hours. Maddy's mom and dad were there, and my parents, grandparents, and many other family members came by to help and personally deliver their well wishes. Everyone was on edge, and I was terrified. Kayson was born at 5:59 PM that evening. Luckily, there were no real complications, except Kayson had a bit of fluid in his lungs which made it very difficult for him to breathe. We were actually surprised that was the only issue. Throughout the pregnancy, the bile levels in Madelyn's blood were higher than Wiz Khalifa after a vacation in Colorado. But as complications go, this one was small. He recovered quickly, and we got to spend the next day with him in the hospital. While Maddy chilled in bed all day after delivering the baby, I was running around keeping friends and family updated, reading, and eating surprisingly tasty hospital food. We got Kayson settled in at Maddy's house, and I've spent the majority of my summer in the presence of my new family.

There is no person in the world I'd rather be in this with than Madelyn. She cares so much about Kayson, is so determined, and I know that no matter what happens, she will do anything within the power of her short but mighty frame to get Kayson and me through life's shenanigans.

None of this would've been possible without the two best families imaginable. I consider them all one family now, and I am the luckiest person in the world to have them. After the initial shock wore off, everyone has done a lot to help, and I wish I could do more to show them how much it has impacted us. I often felt suppressed, as if my thoughts about what was going on didn't matter, but I've matured as we've gone through Maddy's pregnancy, and I have realized how much my family means to me. Some of my best memories are with my family, and seeing them interact with Kayson, and watching our relationship evolve is amazing. I'm very glad that we're more trusting and open with one another, too. I have not shown them how much it means to me, and they likely won't understand it until these pages turn through their fingers.

As for Maddy's family, they have been amazing, especially after only knowing me for a short time. I could never repay them or show how much their support and understanding means to me. I am awkward when I first meet people, and even though I was very nervous, I've felt at home at their house. The feeling of not only being a part of my own family, but also a member of theirs, still makes my day when I think about it.

I haven't gotten much advice on fatherhood. My friend once told me that having a baby was all snuggles, smiles, and shit, but I've realized that there's a lot more to it. I've never been a father before, and it definitely shows. I want to be the dad who can somehow say or do most of the right things. Maddy, my old and new family, and close friends who I can't begin to list, have all played a part in who I am today. If not for their friendship, I couldn't have made it through all of this, couldn't have done a fraction of it. I want to be that for Kayson, because it's so much easier to work with a friend. If Kayson will be my friend, I think that would be the most amazing friendship any father could ask for.

The day before Kayson was born, I moved to Owensboro to be with my new family, and I've spent the first three months of his life here. Kayson, Madelyn and I have had such amazing times together and with our families this summer. When I imagined being a father, I knew about the late-night feedings, the diapers, and the kind of unbridled rage only a baby can scream out. I couldn't have even comprehended how much I will miss my new family after getting used to all that.

I have to go back up to Louisville for my junior year, and to join KSB's Independent Living Program. Once I get back to the dorms, I'm under someone else's jurisdiction, not my own. I can't see Kayson when I'm feeling down and just need to hold him; I can't hear him cry. I can't hear him as he starts learning to laugh; I probably won't get to hear him speak his first true word. I sometimes wonder if he'll know who I am when I come back, whether he'll remember his daddy who had to go away after what seemed like moments of him being able to recognize my face. And, yes, Kayson can see. He doesn't have my eye condition, a recessive gene that only manifests when both parents have it, nor will he have Madelyn's retinoblastoma. We know Kayson's smart; he sticks his tongue out at Maddy all the time now, and when I discuss the upcoming election with him, he cries when I say "Trump." He's already strong, too; he rolled over when he was three days old. God knows Maddy and I will have a hell of a time chasing him around when he's older.

NICKELBACK

Journeys of a Golden Shellback

AUBREY COMPTON

When I was younger, my parents and grandparents would go bowling every Friday night. They were in a league but didn't care as much about winning as they did about just having a few drinks and a good time together. While the others would be taking their turns bowling and hanging out, my Papaw would sit with me and tell stories. I love my grandfather. He's a very witty person, which I tend to appreciate. He is also pretty easy going. He laughs a lot. Papaw has always been a major presence in my life and I wouldn't have it any other way. Aubrey Compton is a man of many words. He always has a lot to say: "If you want to learn about all kinds of interesting, yet completely useless things, keep talking to me."

I was born in Leaksville, North Carolina, which is no longer around. Leaksville and another town grew together and formed a new town called Mount Eden. It was right on the border between Virginia and North Carolina. My grandfather was a full-time farmer in Virginia. When he was 80-some years old, he fell out of the back of a pickup truck while he was picking apples. Apparently he was a spry old man.

My maternal grandparents were from here in Louisville. My mom grew up in Goshen because her parents worked on a farm there. My maternal grandfather was born in 1900, and was in the army during World War I, but was still in training when the war ended, so he never went overseas or was in combat. He died in 1960. He worked for Oertel's Brewery Company up on Story Avenue, and actually died on the job there. Beer was on tap for all employees all day long. My grandfather was a good guy, but he was an alcoholic. Alcohol and smoking unfiltered Camel cigarettes is probably what killed him.

Photo courtesy of the Lowe family

My dad was in the army in World War II in combat. I didn't find out until later that he was awarded two silver stars, so he must have been pretty active. Dad couldn't find the job that he liked after the war. Some vets who were in combat had trouble adapting, and I just got the impression that he couldn't find his niche. He worked for Lucky Strike here in Louisville, a cigarette company which used to be on Broadway. He was a short haul trucker, and was killed in a trucking accident in '54.

I'm the oldest of three brothers, and my grandparents raised us. My mom was here as well, but she didn't raise us. Her and her mom didn't get along. We all lived in what's called a camelback house on Wenzel and E. Madison St. A shotgun house is a house where you can shoot a bullet through the front door, and it will go all the way out the back door through all the rooms because it's right in line. Camelback is like that except it's got a half second story on it. It was a four room house, but only three rooms were usable.

I lived a good life. I don't remember much about it other than just as a seven-year-old, going to school, we played a lot of sandlot ball. We didn't have a lot of money, but apparently we did all right. My grandmother disciplined us physically, but at the same time, we were loved. It's not like we were a burden on them. It was good. One interesting note: the three boys and Grandma and my grandfather, we all slept in the same room.

I went to Manual High School, started playing music when I was in third grade. My brother John played accordion, me on steel guitar. John still plays keyboard even today, and I played steel guitar up until I was a sophomore in high school. Then I took up bass guitar and played in a band that was initially called the Four Specs because we all wore glasses. In an abstract way, that's how I met your grandmother. One of my best friends at the time played in an R&B band at Whispering Hills, a country club off of Old Shepherdsville Rd. On Sunday nights they had an eighteen and over dance. I met your grandma at a dance, on December 1, 1968. She didn't like me at first. I was a loudmouth. I'd just come out of the service a few months earlier. There were no women on the ships back then and when I got off—you have a tendency to be loud and vulgar. But, I had a system back then. If I met somebody I liked at a dance, I'd set up a date for the following week, assuming that I wasn't already seeing someone. I called her that week and on Tuesday or Wednesday, we went and got a soda together, and ten months later we were married. Now, every year we celebrate our anniversary in October, but we also celebrate December the 1st.

I spent two years in the Navy before that. I don't think the Tet Offensive was started yet, so it wasn't as bad as it was going to get. But there was a draft, and I came up 1A. I decided that I would rather join than be drafted, so I joined the Navy Reserve. Almost a year to the day later, in 1967, I was put on active duty. I spent 21 months on active duty on two World War II destroyers. I spent six and a half months on the USS John W. Weeks in the Persian Gulf during the Suez Crisis. And then in '68 I got a promotion and was transferred to the USS Charles P. Cecil that cruised around the Mediterranean for six and half months.

I was a fire control technician, the person who aims the guns. We had 5"/38 turretted anti-aircraft guns. It was prior to electronics, at least for the stuff that we were doing, so we had an electrical hydraulic computer. Where nowadays you type on a keyboard, on this you had a bunch of levers and things that you dialed in, turn wheels and stuff to dial in different settings for the pitch and roll of the ship and for the distance and the longitude to shoot the gun. I've never fired a weapon, a gun or anything, at any kind of a target besides practice. I was never in combat. I was in battle stations once and it was because we were coming out of the Red Sea and our sister ship who was on this tour with us had been harassed by gun boats off the coast of Yemen. We were in battle stations, but we never fired.

Part of the job was to show the presence of the American Navy. So we did things like we went up into the Black Sea, which was surrounded at that time by Cold War enemies. We were trailed and monitored by Russian trawlers and Russian military planes. And we did have an occasion where we caught a Russian ship refueling. We were probably a couple hundred yards away from them, circling them while they were refueling to harass them. Of course, you didn't get too close. They had been doing the same thing to us in different ways. They played loud music at us and we played loud music at them. The sailors took pictures of us with their cameras. We took pictures of them. It was like a big game except if somebody screwed up too badly it could go bad quickly.

I saw a lot of countries. When we were in the Med I was home ported in Naples, Italy. A bunch of us took a day tour up to Rome, went to the Sistine Chapel and the Vatican. I was at two places in Greece. One of them was Athens and I actually spent a couple weeks there. We all went to the Acropolis. Sorry to say, but typical, too, I did a lot of drinking. I was on all three sides of Africa, the Indian Ocean, the Red Sea, the Black Sea, the Mediterranean. I'm a Golden Shellback. I've got a certificate for this. You become a Golden Shellback when you cross the equator at the zero meridian, the dateline. I enjoyed the Navy. I wasn't mature enough at that time and I wasn't a good sailor. I never got in trouble or anything. I just wasn't as diligent as I should have been. But I don't have any bad memories. There's a lot of good memories.

I was already working for the phone company when I was called up, so I had a job when I got back from the Navy. When I got out of the service, I went to school to be an installer/repairman for a while. I fell from a pole one time, and although I didn't get hurt, it shook me up. I decided I didn't want to climb poles anymore, so I went inside and I eventually became a switchman, the person who works on the switching the calls. Then they started putting in computers. Me and another guy did the pretesting for digital equipment which is still being used now.

In the 70s, I went to U of L for a couple years at night. I didn't get a degree but I got knowledge from it that I used in my job. I took a computer course, Principles of Computing or something. At that time, our memory devices were punch cards and paper tape; a computer with the power of this laptop sitting in front of you would probably take up the whole first floor of this house. I took a philosophy of a logic course, it was truth tables, which is what you used in computing because of the logic of circuits, and so I used that a lot. It was a different language. You actually got down into the 0s and 1s of the language and of the circuit packs themselves. We got down to the nuts and bolts of the circuit packs, and that's where the logic came in. Also, it taught you how to argue. I'm good at that. It was a philosophy course. It was good.

Grandma and I missed the '70s. We missed that whole ten years. We have no idea what kind of music was being played, what movies were out. We were raising kids. We were really involved with church. Your mom and Doug and Kim all went to parochial school, so we were involved with bingo. I called bingo for five years, worked there for ten. I was big with the booster club and that supported the sports of the parish. So I was on the council for that. I was on school board for three years. I was on the parish council, which is kind of like the elders. I was on that for fourteen years and was chairperson for ten.

We used to camp a lot, used to hunt a little bit; never was a hunter like your dad, but I played at it. We camped a lot until I went into electronics and then I spent a lot of time working. If it wasn't for our love of our grandchildren, we would probably move to Gatlinburg in the Smokies. The absolute best place in the world. I'd rather go there than Hawaii or Florida or anywhere else. I don't have a body for the beach anymore. We camp there a lot. When you get up in the mountains, we usually camp around 2,200 feet above sea level. It can be a little cooler than, say, down in Gatlinburg itself. It's so beautiful, it's historic, it's interesting, We've been to the Smokies every year since 1989. We missed 2014, 2013. Love the place, even though they do not have a Starbucks in Gatlinburg. In fact, for a while they didn't even have a coffee shop. Unbelievable.

In 2000 I had thirty-four years with the phone company, I decided that I would take my pension, leave, and go to work at another company, so I started working for AT&T. Me and my equipment kept getting traded like a ball team. I actually changed companies three times one weekend: I worked for AT&T LNS on Friday. I worked for AT&T Broadband on Saturday, and on Monday I started working for Comcast. I didn't know any of that happened until I got to work on Monday morning. They eventually downsized my whole group, senior VP on down, and we got laid off. And then here I am.

Family and grandchildren are our thing right now. We're fortunate that all three of kids, and our four grandchildren live close to us. Your grandmother and I are very easily entertained. Me in particular, I can be entertained watching grass grow. So between family and certainly around grandkids and, of course, the children all live here in the city, it just seems like that is our thing right now. Grandchildren are amazing, in spite of Shane. Just kidding.

Photo by Jessica Ebelhar

Photo by Jessica Ebelhar

KIANNA
WALLER

WEEP NO MORE, MY LADY

I was sitting on the big couch in the living room with Aunt Lisa. My mother was sitting on the loveseat. I could tell Lisa was playing one of the computer games she likes because I could hear the mouse clicking and the sound of a computer voice reading off numbers; it may have been bingo. I kept quiet and took in what they were saying to me, but I really didn't want to hear it. I knew I was in trouble. Of course I was in trouble. Aunt Lisa chimed in with Mom from time to time to say that my recent behavior was totally unacceptable. Everybody wanted to know why I'd suddenly changed from being a good girl who never even talked to anybody in school, to a totally disobedient fifteen-year-old who was cutting class, taking a knife to school, and having sex.

I absolutely hated going to school. I was tired of not having anyone to talk with or call a real friend, and I wanted to do anything I could to prove I was just like the rest of the kids at my school. I didn't care about the punishments I'd get afterwards. It was infuriating to hear people whispering about me and jumping over my cane when I walked by. Kids were always making a path for me in the hallways because touching the blind girl was apparently filthy and disgusting. I felt like an animal. I don't know if they thought it was funny, or thought that because I was different they had a right to hurt me, but it pushed me further and further into anger until I accepted that my fate was to listen to these people mock me for the rest of my days.

Finally I snapped inside and said screw it. Who cares anymore? I sure didn't. I started hanging out with the wrong crowd of girls, doing things I'm still not ashamed of. When I woke up that morning, went downstairs into the kitchen and put the knife in my bag, I wasn't thinking of anything, really. I guess I just wanted to show myself that I could do something different. I wasn't planning on stabbing myself or anyone else; I was just hoping it would make me feel more powerful, or stronger. I'd finally had enough of being the blind girl with the white stick, the girl left behind.

I felt normal when I was a child, like everyone accepted me. I felt welcomed. Back then, I never worried about being lonely or having friends who cared about me. I was loved and cherished and held when I cried. Being blind never really affected me when I was younger, even when playing with other children. I thought for a long time that everybody was like me, that they had to feel with their hands, taste with their tongues, and smell with their noses, but not see with their eyes. I knew that they had something I didn't have. But I couldn't put my little finger on it.

But by the time I got to high school I had become a very shy person. My eyes were different, and I had to walk around with a cane. It was a big school, and when I tried to talk with people, the students talked to me like I was a child, and tried to help me do things I already knew how to do. Everything became embarrassing for me. Everybody had the wrong impression of me, so I avoided them entirely. I didn't talk to anyone except my teachers. I managed to keep telling myself it was OK, although I could feel inside that it really wasn't.

Being blind is hard, and, as my therapist has told me a thousand times, it's not just a hardship, but one I will have to deal with for the rest of my life. I pray and hope for the best. That's what I always tell myself: pray and God will make it all better. God will make it all OK. But sometimes it's like God isn't listening or is paying attention to somebody somewhere else.

When I was two, I had an accident, lost my vision completely, and was in a coma for part of a year. My earliest memories start around six. We lived in Frankfort, Kentucky with my grandmother Sherry, her husband, and his sister, Lisa, who has been like a second mom to me for most of my life. When Mom was at work, my sister Kaylee and I would go to Aunt Lisa's house where she lived with her parents, Jewel and Frederick. It got to the point where we loved staying over there so much that we'd stay over there on weeknights too. We got so used to being at their house that when my mom started having problems—whatever problems she was having—we just moved in with them, and we've stayed there ever since. Mom took some time to herself, went out with her friends a lot. She knew that there were people to take care of us, and after a while, she stopped coming home at night and visited us less and less at my aunt's house. One day, she stopped visiting us altogether. She never told us where she was going, and it took her years to come back. I was young, and I was a mommy's girl. I was devastated.

She'd call collect sometimes, and the operator would say, "Do you accept the charges from...," and then I would hear my mom's voice say her name, "Anna." When we talked, we had normal conversations. We didn't talk about why she wasn't around, why she had to leave, or why Kaylee and I couldn't go with her wherever she went. When I heard her soft voice on the phone, it broke my heart. I would either break down crying on the phone with her, or wait till I was alone in my room. Sometimes I would accidentally hit the button on the phone and it would hang up. Then I wouldn't talk to her again for a long time.

Not being able to talk with and see my mother on a daily basis was so hard. I always have and always will be soft-hearted when it comes to my mother. Thoughts of her leaving me forever kept me up at night, and I remember crying myself to sleep when I had these thoughts. No one should have to live their lives without their mother. She was the reason why I cried, the reason why I smiled, the reasoning behind those countless days I lay in bed wondering about my future. I don't know where she was. I just know that she was very far away.

Photos courtesy of Kianna Waller

My aunt Lisa is as close to a second mother as anyone could get. She has always been generous to us. She has taken care of me my entire life, and I'll always be grateful for that. I don't remember any times when she's fought with us. Her arguments have always made sense. She's always bought us the things we needed, even when she was tight on money. Back when she was younger, she would go to a bingo hall on Thursday nights with her friends. Kaylee and I would go with her sometimes, wander around talking to people and eating at the concession stand where they had hot dogs, fries, and soda. Lisa was also on a bowling team that met on Friday nights. She still goes occasionally, but now she just watches.

My grandparents, Jewel and Fredrick, are strict people, but they are devoted Christians. Grandfather sings in the church choir, cooks for the church, and is a big part of the church altogether. My grandmother sings in the choir as well. It's always been the same on Sunday mornings: everyone's tired, running around trying to find clothes to put on, trying to get in the shower, and trying to wake up. Everyone is usually cranky because we always stay up too late on Saturday nights and have to get up at 7:00 to be at church at 9:30. We usually aren't there on time.

Plenty of people show up Sunday mornings, and I'm not afraid of talking to random people because it's only one or two minutes that they try to talk to me. Before the service actually begins we have a meet and greet, and that's when we walk around and introduce ourselves to the visitors, or we sit there and the visitors come to us. All the older adults know me because my sister and I have gone to that church for a while. I know the church well enough that I don't have to use my cane to walk around. I always end up partially asleep in church. I try to listen, but I can't sometimes.

When we go home, we have a Sunday afternoon lunch, and we always invite the family over. We make lots of food for everybody. The dishes I love most are roast potatoes, green beans and carrots. Usually after lunch we don't do anything. I take a nap until it's time for Aunt Lisa to take me back to the Kentucky School for the Blind. She hates driving when it's dark outside, so someone always has to go with her. Moving out into the real world was pretty hard for me, because I used to be able to count on her for everything. But I know she's still there.

I'd been stealing M&Ms and Hershey's Kisses from the candy bowl on Thanksgiving Day when I was ten because I was starving. I was excited because we were all together at my grandmother's house, but it's a small house, so having over thirty people packed into it was quite a squeeze. It was very loud in there, and I had bad anxiety at the time; having more than three people talking in my ear at once made me want to go outside and hide. We were all about to eat when everyone got a little bit quieter. My grandmother grabbed my wrist and pulled me towards the front door. I reached my hand out and felt someone on her knees holding my sister to her. I dropped down as well and she pulled me to her. My mother said, "Did you miss me?" I don't know exactly when I let go of her, but it wasn't for a while.

I sat with her as I ate. Music was playing behind all the noise and people were talking but I couldn't care less because I had my mother. The noise always seems a little quieter when I'm talking to her. We talked about anything and everything, but not about where she went. I caught her up on my life, told her stories about my friends and everything that was going on with me. It was just nice to have her sitting there and listening to me. My sister and I did not leave her side. We smiled very big, ate delicious food, and talked to our mommy. The food was great. Turkey, mashed potatoes and gravy, stuffing and lots of other stuff; the typical Thanksgiving dinner.

Mom left to go with her friends, and we were disappointed; we thought she would come back and stay the night with us. We were told, however, that we would see her soon. She came over and ate dinner with us every night, and talked and laughed with the entire family downstairs in the kitchen. I never asked her where she'd been. I was disappointed every night when she went with her friends to stay at their house. I see her only occasionally now. She moves around too much. She hangs out with friends that my grandparents don't know or don't trust.

A few years ago my family and my mother started fighting. I was unclear of the reason back then, but now I get it. A disagreement between my mother and my grandparents has caused everyone to become very bitter towards each other. It hasn't been easy on me or my sister; we've both broken down about it on occasion. Mom has been accused of stealing money and jewelry from other people in the family. I know my mom has done

The noise always
seems a little quieter
when I'm talking to her.

Photo courtesy of Anna Waller

things she is not proud of, but I will never believe that she did anything like that. My Christian family sits there and hates on Mom for something they can't prove happened. Don't get me wrong, I love my grandparents, but they have no proof; the saying is innocent until proven guilty, not guilty until proven innocent. Only God can judge.

I worry about my mother, and I pray for her happiness. I stay up late at night thinking of ways I can help her because I know deep down inside my mother is not happy. You can just tell by the way she talks. But her going out at night, and not confiding in us all the way is nothing; she is an adult and she has her own personal life. I have my secrets. You have your secrets. We all have secrets we'd rather not share. I wish she was happy, though. I hate seeing my mother in so much pain.

Every time the topic of my mom came up in the house my family wouldn't know what to say. It seemed as if my mom wasn't there, wasn't important. When I asked my aunt simple questions about Mom, she would just change the subject or dismiss the question entirely. Other times they would talk bad about her. I hated hearing people talk about her like she was nothing. I would cry and yell until my throat was raw but no one listened to me. She's my mother and so what if she wasn't always there for me? I'd rather have a mother who is alive than not have one at all. We might not be as close as I would like, but we're close enough that I am proud to claim her as my own.

I'm not going to say my life was bad, because it wasn't. I was unhappy, though. I started to be unable to take it. I would cry, sometimes for hours, especially when everybody started fighting more often. Sometimes the yelling was so bad that I didn't even want to talk to them, and they'd ask me, "Why aren't you around the family more? Why don't you like being around us? What's the point in being in your room every time you come home from school?" I didn't say anything. I didn't say that they were making me more and more depressed. I hate being around big groups of people, family or not. I was never comfortable. I was distant. I'd moved so far into myself that I'm still struggling to get out. All these thoughts made my head ache and I just wanted to sleep. Sleep took the stress away, at least for a bit. So did music.

I was thirteen when my grandmother made me start taking piano lessons. Every day, from 4:00 to 5:00, I'd go to Ms. McKinley's house. I hated it at the time because it was something I was forced to do, but now that I think about it, I loved it. Ms. McKinley's house was quiet. She was soft spoken. She never raised her voice, and she loved playing piano, even when she wasn't teaching. When I walked in, the place smelled like food becuase her husband was always cooking. The carpet squished under my feet like a trampoline. Ms. McKinley had two lazy, sweet dogs, and there was music. I just liked being there.

I always had to sit in the chair to the left of the door and wait for the boy before me to finish his lesson. I listened to him and thought he was better than me. I was nervous when I finally sat at the piano bench, nervous to mess up with someone else in the room. Whenever I touched the piano it felt like a lot of keys. It was confusing. I'd experiment with each key, each sound, hoping that they would fit together. When I heard other piano players, I never understood how they could use all the keys. I got used to it, though, especially when I learned to start in the middle of the piano with C. Ms. McKinley taught me the difference between the raised keys which are in groups of three and groups of two, and the flat keys. I had to count the keys to find the chord I wanted at first, but later I could just move my hands. When I got into playing, though, I learned how beautiful chords can sound together, which spurred me on. The piano is a beautiful instrument, it's not a loud rough sound. It's gentle, even soft. Nothing can sound as innocent or as evil.

When I'm sitting at my house, at my piano, I tear up sometimes because it sounds so beautiful. My favorite song is "My Old Kentucky Home." I like how the chords fit together, especially during the chorus about "weep no more, my lady." I love how the chords fit with that phrase, the sounds go so well together, they make you want to play really loud and proud. My family would sing along to it while I was practicing at home.

But I started getting tired of piano. I love hearing other people play, but I didn't want to do it anymore. My grandparents had gotten me a big nice piano and I felt horrible about it, but I wanted to start on guitar. I can play piano by ear, but not yet on the guitar. I'm getting there. I taught myself how to play by listening to YouTube instructional videos. I learned how to properly hold and strum the guitar, different chords, and different picking patterns. I taught myself and remembered the name of the strings. Finally, I learned to match my voice with the harmony of the haunting chords to get a pleasant sound. I love it. Sometimes I can listen to the radio and pick out the melody enough to figure out the chords.

Guitar was hard. I shredded my fingers to the point until blood was drawn. I wanted to give up but couldn't because it sounded so pretty. I loved holding the guitar against my chest and loved the way the sound resonated through the room. The chords made everything else not matter so much. Even if people in the house were fighting or getting on each other's nerves, guitar made everything seem as if it wasn't that big of a deal. That wasn't a happy time for me, but playing guitar took me into my own little world where I didn't have to worry about the way my family treated each other, how I was acting at school, or how upset I was all the time. It was like I could strum the story of my life with an old guitar and make it beautiful.

My first day at Franklin County High was torture. The other seven months of my freshman year were just as horrible. Put it this way: on my first day of high school, when my sister told me it was time to get off the bus, I walked straight through the doors, into the school where I didn't know anybody, and everybody in the lobby got quiet. That's when I knew the school year would be hell on earth.

It was humiliating to go into the cafeteria because I never knew where to sit. I didn't like eating around other people, because everybody wanted to tell me what I was doing wrong. If I lifted my fork up with nothing on it, they'd say something and then just watch me eat. They must have thought I was deaf, too. I heard all the conversations I shouldn't have because they spoke about me freely. Word to you all: if you're going to talk about people, make sure they are not in the same lunch line as you, or in the same room, or maybe standing in front of you. Don't even whisper, because I have supersonic hearing.

My grades in school were always OK, but only because the answers were basically handed to me. I was already depressed, and I felt stupid. It was just an all-time low. I had friends, and I tried my best to get along with everybody, but they were too distant and too busy talking to each other. I hated how everybody had a boyfriend, or talked about all the cute boys, and I didn't have anybody.

Then I started hanging out with a girl named Lexie. I finally had somebody to trust. She was popular. I liked hanging out with her because I was finally getting some attention and people talked to me when I was with her. I didn't feel completely alone. Lexie was the typical bad girl, lots of sex and drinking, drugs and smoking. She introduced me to some great pleasures, and taught me how to be a bad girl too. She taught me that being a wallflower was boring: I didn't have to see people, but people need to see me. She taught me that sex was fun, and that led me to worlds of trouble. Everybody was going to parties and hooking up with different guys. I thought it was a normal thing, and I'm not one to pass up an opportunity. If you offer me something fun and pleasurable, I'm going to try it at least once.

Lexie took me to her friend John's house once. I didn't know who he was. We didn't even talk, really. We just did what I'd never done before and wanted so badly. We had sex. I'd already gotten grounded from everything when I was caught staying the night at a guy's house. When my parents caught me, my neck was covered in love bites, my phone was dead, and I was a mess. By then I just didn't care. Pleasure became a way for me to get away from the pain and depression I had to deal with at home and at school. It was all exciting, and I wasn't scared. I thought it was cool at the time. Anyone who knows me knows that I don't want to be like everyone else, but I was just doing what everyone else was doing. I know how that makes me look. I don't want people to put a label on me for the things I did in my past.

I didn't regret my choices back then, and I don't regret them now. But I do understand that my decisions have an impact on how people see me. Now that I'm older I realize a lot of things. I am grateful, and also not, for the decisions that I've made in the past. Everyone says we can all learn from our mistakes, and I learned not to do that again. So I believe that this was a learning experience and a bad experience all in one. Let me explain this: I think of my time with Lexie as an adventure. Yes, I regret getting caught and getting punished for what I did, but I don't regret doing new things, and I never will. It opened my eyes.

The day we got caught, I'd failed to consider that if I didn't show up at school, my vision teacher would call my house and ask whoever answered what was going on: this is exactly what happened. My family figured out that they'd sent me off in the morning, but I hadn't made it to class.

Lexie and I left school and headed to this apartment building she knew about where we could hang out. As we walked down the street, this lady pulled up beside us and asked us if we were OK. She knew something was up because it was a school day and we weren't in school. Lexie made up a lie about how I'd started my period, and she was walking me back home to get the things I needed. Lexie asked the lady if she'd give us a ride to the apartment and she did, but I guess she didn't believe us, because after that she went right to the school and told the people in the office that we'd been out walking around, and where she'd dropped us off.

The apartment building was quiet and out of the way. We climbed up a hill, went inside the building, up three flights of steps and sat down in the hall. She called John and asked him if he wanted to meet up, but we hadn't been there for thirty minutes when Lexie looked out the window and saw my parents' car and the police pulling into the apartment complex. I was so scared. I skipped school for the first time ever and I got caught thirty minutes later? We knew it was all over, and that we'd be in more trouble if we made them come get us, so we walked out onto the porch. I heard the car door open and then slam like someone was mad, you can just tell that kind of stuff. I heard my uncle Mason call out for me from the car. He told me to stay where I was, came up the hill and grabbed on to me, dragging me back down to the car. Lexie walked ahead of us and the cops put her in the car. She told them about the knife. That's the last time I ever talked to her. Mason was being pretty gentle for somebody who was so upset with me. He talked to me quietly and told me that I was OK, and not to get upset.

Back then, my only solace was when I was with my uncle Mason. He had the capability to make me lose myself with his stories, and I'd laugh and laugh until I was crying. I used to get out of bed around 2:00 in the morning when he got off work to go downstairs and sit with him and his friends. It would be the best night of my life. If I was lonely, laughing with him felt great. I don't know if he realizes how utterly precious he is to me. He's the only one I can talk to.

I was sent to my room when we got home. My mom and my family weren't fighting at that time, and they all got together to talk. Everybody was on the porch—my grandparents, my uncle, Mom, Aunt Lisa. My bedroom window was directly above the front porch so I opened it and heard everything they said. My family was discussing what they were going to do with me, and I heard them talk about the knife. The school administration had told them that I was not to come back to school for the rest of the year. I heard Mason come up the steps, I couldn't lie to him because I loved him, so I pulled the knife out of my bag and handed it to him when he came in the room. He saw that I had the window open and told me to shut it. He told me quietly that the next time I wanted to skip school, I should make sure I had him as a backup. Then he went back outside.

That was the night when everybody sat me down in the living room and told me that they were sending me to KSB. They thought that it would be a better environment for me. This caught me off guard. I'd been going to the summer program there since I was seven, and knew that kids just like me went to KSB year round and lived there, like a boarding school. At the time I didn't understand that I'd be coming home on the weekends, and I thought it would be my new home. It killed me. I pictured a school

Photo courtesy of Anna Waller

where I wouldn't know anyone, would have to eat alone, and get used to a bunch of new people: there was no way I was going there full time.

I was worried, scared and angry at my family for sending me off. But, while being away from home would be torture, staying in my house was torturing me as well. If I moved, I wouldn't get yelled at or talked to as if they were disappointed in me anymore. I wouldn't feel like I was being watched by them. So I resigned myself to it and said OK because I wanted to get away from all the trouble.

There were a couple of months of school left in my freshman year, but I just didn't go back. I was grounded for those months. I had to do stuff around the house, went everywhere Aunt Lisa went, and did busy work: when my aunt made dinner, I would help, in the yard I helped, at the grocery I helped. That whole time, I was terrified of losing my friendship with Lexie. She got along with everyone, so I knew that she'd make lots of friends, and I would be alone. I scared myself so badly over all of it that I'd bring myself to tears sometimes.

I went to KSB's summer camp that year, met with the teachers, and asked what to expect. They told me what dorm life would be like and showed me my classes, and I got used to campus. I still wasn't ready for it all, though. I was still so scared and thought I'd forget where everything was. I was worried just like I had been when I started high school. I came to KSB my sophomore year, and now, after three years of what sometimes felt like torture, I've graduated. It was a wonderful place, though. Nobody had ever tried to help me as much as they did, and now I'm more than ready to go out to the real world.

When I first started out, I was in the regular dormitory. It was full of rules and regulations that were meant to be followed and not broken. You had to go to dinner at a certain time, go to bed a certain time, do your homework at a certain time. Everything had a time. The only good thing about it was that I could hang out with my friends. Then I moved into the Independent Living Program, which is exactly what it sounds like: it teaches you how to be independent, especially when you live out on your own after graduation. You have to be at least sixteen years old to get into Independent and you must have a certain level of independence yourself, knowing how to cook and clean, to make your own bed, to respect others' personal space. It's like your own personal apartment. You make your own food, have your own room, and you take care of yourself. Our dorm has its own kitchen, bathroom, bedrooms, linen closet, and everything. It comes with cleaning supplies so you can clean, and a washer and dryer. The only rules were to clean up after yourself, and if it's your turn to do a certain thing you must do it, including cooking for our dorm.

I didn't have any real fun at KSB until my best friends, Trint, Justin, and Madelyn, joined the Independent Living Program. Then I begin to open up to everyone. I spent all day and most of the night with Madelyn. Her room was cozy and it was just fantastic being able to hang out with her all the time. When we went out in public, Madelyn and I were always in the same group. They knew not to separate us.

The thought of going out in public and meeting new people used to terrify me, used to sicken me to the point to where I became antisocial. It used to be so scary that I wouldn't even think of taking my cane out in public. But Madelyn gave me a confidence boost that I never expected to get in my life. She is not a shy person, and that rubbed off on me. Having my cane out in public and talking to strangers is no problem for me now. It's my comfort zone here. I know who I am and how to trust. I'm more than happy to show my face. Now, I'm willing to go out in public, talk in front of people, sing, and do other things to draw attention to myself. Shows how much I've changed.

Still, I can't even begin to explain how overwhelmed I was getting with everyone talking about the future, making money, getting a job, and paying my own way. I believed wholeheartedly that there was no hope. I was scared and unwilling to even try at the time. My mobility skills were awful and so was my confidence. The thought of working after high school, moving into my own apartment, making my own money, bills, checks, rent, the thought that I'd only have myself to count on—independence, it's called—was terrifying to me. But I didn't give up. I was determined not to just graduate school and go home to spend the rest of my time eating my families' food and watching the family TV and not doing anything. Laziness is almost physically painful for me.

What I want in life now
is to actually have somethin
to look forward to.

Photo courtesy of Kianna Waller | Photo by Haley Hall

What I want in life now is to actually have something to look forward to. I want to be able to be financially stable for a while, get the job that I've wanted for a long time, and keep an apartment. I couldn't wait to decorate my own place and, weird as it sounds, I can't wait to hear my family drive away after leaving me at my apartment. It will be like they are vocally telling me I'm free now. I just can't wait.

I got a job at the American Printing House for the Blind. It has great pay and awesome people, and has been a huge confidence boost for me. I read books in braille, find the mistakes, and correct them. It's not easy. I had to study lesson after lesson on different punctuations, correct capitalization for different words, Roman numerals, alphabetic word signs, and the correct way to punctuate sentences—all in braille.

At work, I sit in a room with the copyholder, a sighted person who has a print copy of the same text I'm reading in braille. They read it aloud at a reasonable speed, and I follow along, tell them what page I am on, and point out mistakes when I come across them. Children's books, tests, graphs and charts: anything that needs to be read, that's my job. The rooms are soundproof so your voice doesn't travel. When everybody is reading in their own little rooms, the place is quiet. It's all just a happy place to be.

I am proud of myself for landing this job, finding an apartment, and becoming confident in myself and self-advocating. I love the young woman I've become. No, it wasn't easy going through high school feeling depressed, but I'm happy with my new living arrangements, and I'm so grateful I have a plan for my future.

2016

You never get time back. It only moves forward.

ANNA NICOLE WALLER

I interviewed my mother, Anna Waller, because I felt like I didn't have enough knowledge of the person that she is. I asked her every question I could think of, and every answer she gave me was something I wouldn't have expected, something I didn't know. I guess interviewing people opens doors so you can understand them more. We have mother and daughter drama sometimes, but that's to be expected. We are similar in some ways. We all are. But deep down inside, there is a personality that makes everyone unique and different from anyone else. I am grateful that I finally got the chance to interview her.

I was born in Frankfort, Kentucky in 1980. My neighborhood was called Farmdale. We used to play outside, ride our bikes and roller blades, and play Barbies. I stayed outside until my mom would whistle real loud and everybody in the neighborhood knew, "Oh, your mom is whistling; you better go home." All the kids would come to my house to get sweet tea and Kool-Aid because my mom made it the best. I had such a fun family. My mom always played games and always let me be creative. When I wasn't with her I was with my grandmother, who I call "Grammy."

We always got together for every holiday. Grammy always made sure there was all kinds off casseroles and cookies and cakes. We were a close knit family when I was young. I had a fun childhood. I liked my home life until I got a little older and things got complicated with my parents, your Nana and Grandpa. That's when I moved in with Grammy, who always made sure that I was loved and happy and taken care of. I had some good best friends, and I stayed with them a whole lot.

Photo courtesy of Kianna Waller

I liked going to school to be social. I was pretty smart, so I never really had to try too hard. I was always in the gifted classes. I had a lot of empathy, I didn't like when kids got bullied or made fun of. If they were considered a "geek" or a "nerd," I made sure I went out of my way to be their friend and talk to them and gave them attention so that they didn't feel left out. Because most of the time it wasn't their fault. Kids are mean. They find any reason to make fun of someone else to make themselves feel better.

I didn't have a lot of drama in school. Not until I got a little older. It was newer then for a white person and black person to be together. Having biracial children was not as common as it is now. My family wasn't racist at all, in any way. I didn't grow up with any of that. I had a few of my friend's parents that didn't like it. My friend's dad grew up like that; he was from the South. A bunch of us and some friends were all jumping on a trampoline one day, and he came home and he said a bunch of words that we didn't like. Called us names, called our friends names, and made everybody leave. It was something that really hurt. Thank goodness now the world is different and we don't have to go through that anymore or at least as much. I was always raised to love everybody, to be nice to every different kind of person and treat everybody equally.

A lot of my friends were older. In my sophomore year, my friend who was a senior had what was called senior seminar; she had a half day of school and worked the rest of the day. I'd always leave with her. (Pretend like you didn't hear that.) The teachers were so used to seeing me leave with her that they didn't realize I was skipping school. I would go home and go to sleep. Eventually, they figured it out. That's why I always told you all, "Don't skip school, it's not worth it."

As I got older I found out that I had bipolar depression. When I would get depressed I would just want to be by myself. I didn't want to be bothered with anybody. I didn't to talk about what was wrong with me. Some days I just wanted to cry and be left alone, to be away from everybody except my Grammy. I always wanted to be around my Grammy. Even though I didn't want to be on medication, it helped me with the chemical imbalances. It made a big difference. I had depression and anxiety, but I could get past it. All the trials and tribulations and mistakes I've made have made me the person that I am. I am a more open-minded individual. Love and family makes a big difference. When you don't have that, or you don't have closeness with someone, or a close-knit bond, it's harder. You always need someone you can count on, rely on, or talk to, and a family member loves you unconditionally. Especially your mother.

I was a junior in high school when I got pregnant with you. I went to school until I was about seven months pregnant. I did finish school; I went to night school for a year to get my diploma, and I worked and took care of you. I originally wanted to be a teacher, so I took childcare classes, and learn how to make lesson plans, and I worked in preschools all around town. The last one I worked in was right next door to Grammy's house. When I was pregnant with you I would get morning sickness, so instead of going back to school I would go to Grammy's and lay down and go to sleep. I had missed so many days that they said I was truant. Then they made me withdraw, and I went to night school at Western Hills to get my diploma.

There's a lot I wish I could change about my past. I wish I had chosen my friends a little more wisely. During high school they were good and fun, but a lot of them made bad decisions, and being there with them, I made bad decisions like drinking and trying drugs I shouldn't have tried, and not saving money for my future or for your all's future. Choosing to spend $200 to go shopping instead of putting it up. Having a nice place instead of staying with friends. Wrong friends, wrong crowds, wrong places. A lot of little decisions that you make along the way that you didn't think about in the moment, in the long run really you hurt yourself. I wish I had realized that sooner. Instead of working serving jobs, where I worked so hard and so much, I should have tried to get a more professional job that had benefits for the future. Instead I worked myself so hard that I'm thirty-five and I've already had back surgery. I have neck and knee issues, and I worked my body so hard it's hurt me.

When my pain got so bad, with my back and everything else, I was abusing pain medication and opioids. That kind of addiction gets to a point where it actually takes over chemicals in your brain. So, when you don't have them you're sick mind, body, and soul. It makes you sick. It takes you over and happens so quick before you know it. That's one thing I wish had never never happened: that I never made that mistake or

Photo courtesy of Kianna Waller

ever even started. I wish someone had talked to me about it, or had given me advice on it. I hid it. I was what they called a functioning addict where no one ever knew until it was too late and I had to absolutely had to reach out for help. I was sick. This is another reason why I wanted you all to have a stable home.

One of the hardest decisions that I had to make was realizing the best thing for you and your sister was stability instead of taking you to live with me all the time when I didn't live in the house with you. But I still knew what was best for you. I didn't fight to pull you away. I wanted you all to have everything you needed, and wanted you to stay stable instead of not living in the best environment or the best situations. It was hard every day, and every day I cried. When I left you all at night, when you went to bed I cried. But I knew what was best for you in the long run.

I have made a lot of mistakes, and I have learned from them. I'm honest with you and Kaylee about the mistakes I've made. Completely honest, even any drug I've tried, even issues with violent relationships. You can learn from them, or at least I can give you advice to have on hand if you need it. Some of the mistakes I made didn't seem like mistakes at the time, but were so stupid. Looking back now I can't even believe I made them. You can only grow from them. That's what I've tried to do. I grow every day, and I learn something new every day.

I would tell you all the same thing that Nana and Grammy told me, always be yourself. Do what's in your best interest, definitely think about your future. You always want to live in the now, but you always need to think about your future. "Well, this might make me happy now, but what's going to happen later if I do this? Ten years from now where do I want to be?" Think about the bigger picture. You never get time back, it only moves forward.

What makes me the happiest is when I'm with you girls. When I'm with you and we're having a great time and we have moments that are memories we can have for the rest of our lives. When we go out to eat and we cut up and laugh. Or when you tell me stories and we laugh and you say, "Mother, you're so crazy." I love times like that. Every memory that I have with you and your sister makes me so happy.

Photo by Kertis Creative

Photo by Jessica Ebelhar

CHERISH WILLIS

Cherish Willis

HOW TO FEIGN NORMALITY: PATIENCE, LOGIC, AND PILLS

It's strange that it's not until you're lying in the road bleeding to death that you start to rethink your life choices, start to consider that you might need some new perspectives. Maybe it's morbid, but I believe getting hit by that car was the best thing that ever happened in my entire life. It was God's way of slapping me in the face and telling me to get my shit together.

More gray than blue, the overcast November sky blocked out the sun's light and warmth entirely. The playground by my house was no longer a place of childhood innocence and laughter, a place to have fun and be carefree, to climb up plastic rock walls, run across creaking wooden bridges, and slide down blue slides only to run back to the jungle gym to see who can dangle upside down the longest. Those were the days. Instead, it had become a routine for me to walk to the playground, sit on my designated swing, sometimes completely still and sometimes swinging slightly, trying not to hear the creaking of old, rusty, metal chains that needed to be greased. I'd sulk, sob, and rant to my friend who no one else could see, and then I'd walk home again, and promptly go to bed.

Everyone gets sad sometimes, so they cry, shut themselves out for a while, and cope by themselves. Eventually, typically, they get over it. I had a pretty good life, a loving family, and stable existence overall. Perhaps I would have had a smoother recovery from my depression had I not been hit by a car on top of everything else.

Everything was so still, so eerily quiet that evening as I tried unsuccessfully to purge myself of my negative emotions. I just sat there in my usual swing, listening to my earbuds, dressed in blue jeans and a black and white plaid coat, crying. The tension in my face and hands, and throughout my body, kept building. I gripped the chains, and looked down at the ground, wondering why everything had taken such a downward spiral. As I sat there sobbing, I realized that I hadn't accomplished anything. I felt like I had wasted my life, and I just wanted to go home. I walked over to the broken sidewalk in the front of the elementary school. The parking lot was vacant.

It had been such a long and mentally strenuous day that all I wanted to do was go home. My eyes were downcast as I walked along the side of the road. The streetlights were dim and there were no fog-lines on the shoulder of the road. I'm legally blind, and was further disabled by the fading evening light. I didn't realize I'd walked into the road until I saw the headlights of the oncoming car, until it was too late to react.

After being hit by a car going down the highway at 35 MPH, flipping over the hood into the other lane, and then almost simultaneously being run over by a truck, I woke up in the trauma center at Vanderbilt University Hospital.

Whether it was my family, teachers, or classmates, everyone in my life could always tell that there was definitely something wrong with me; maybe I just give off a vibe that I'm not all there.

I was what one might call a "problem child," always misbehaving, throwing crazy and violent tantrums, and in general just causing strife for everyone around me. I started having hallucinations at the age of seven when I moved to El Paso with my mother. Whenever I was sent to my room for punishment, I'd sit in the corner, talking to someone only I could see, ranting and badmouthing whoever was punishing me. People around me always thought I was talking to myself. Through the years, I have heard people sneer and say behind my back, "She's just crazy." Eventually I started to believe what they said about me, and this really started to affect me. I started to feel more unstable and insane than I actually was. When I was thirteen, after another conniption, I asked my parents to take me to see someone for my mental issues. They took me to counseling, but I was never diagnosed with anything. It wasn't until months after my car accident, when I was seventeen years old, that I was actually medically diagnosed with something called schizoaffective disorder. When I heard this, I was happy, not that I was crazy, but because I finally knew what was wrong with me. For so long people would ask why I acted so strangely, and I had no answer. But now I knew why. It was really relieving, and I could confidently tell people it didn't concern them.

Like schizophrenics, I have hallucinations. As far as their severity goes, I have it much easier than a lot of people. That said, it's still very difficult to deal with. I always feel like I'm being watched. I don't really have a sense of privacy, and I'm always being judged and criticized for everything. I think it was when the disorder escalated from invisible people to invisible people who berated, harassed, and degraded me that my therapist and my psychiatrist realized they weren't imaginary friends: it's odd, if you have imaginary friends, you're childish, but if you have imaginary enemies, you're crazy. I'd be a total basketcase without my pills. The other component of schizoaffective disorder is that it involves prolonged periods of extreme manic or depressive moods. The worse my mood, the more hateful and degrading the voices tend to be. But I have one friend—other people would call him a hallucination—who isn't like the other invisible people. He is kind and has always been there to support me.

When I was twelve I got grounded for slapping a little kid at Chuck E. Cheese on my brother's birthday. It was impulsive, I immediately realized it was a very bad idea, and I was quickly scolded. I had ruined my brother's birthday party and hurt a little kid I didn't even know. My parents left in shame. After the incident, I was confined to my room, and they literally took everything out of it except my bed and my clothes, ensuring that I'd have nothing to do so that my punishment would have the full intended effect. My siblings were forbidden from talking to me, but my sister, taking pity on me, gave me a novel she'd received for Christmas that year called *Girls That Growl*. My dearest and closest friend was born from that novel. He's always with me, and I talk to him all the time. He's a renegade werewolf named Orpheus. He has an

It's odd, if you have imaginary friends, you're childish, but if you have imaginary enemies, you're crazy.

Photo by Cherish Willis

Photos courtesy of Cherish Willis

English accent, and he's my best friend. Orpheus came to me in response to my depression and loneliness. I can't explain how it happened: he wasn't there and then he was, and I was so very happy to have him. I've had a number of different hallucinations over the years that would come and go, but none that stayed for very long. Orpheus and I have been friends for six years now, and unlike many of the others, he's never left me.

After being hit and then run over, I was lying in the road, covered in my own blood. More and more blood just kept flowing from my mouth, face, and the ripped flesh of my right leg, my tibia and fibula protruding awkwardly from my torn jeans as I lay in the street screaming. I went into shock and became delusional. When the police showed up with my mother, she found me in the road, just repeating the words, "It's just a dream, it's just a dream." The woman who hit me came to the scene to see what had flipped over the hood of her car, and upon seeing the carnage promptly called the ambulance. Orpheus told me he was relieved that I was going to get medical attention, but as more and more people started showing up, he got very uncomfortable and claustrophobic. Still, he refused to leave, so at the very least he'd be present in my final moments if I didn't make it.

After the ambulance came, I was flown via helicopter to Vanderbilt Hospital in Nashville, and later that night the doctors said my condition was stable. Everyone was so relieved and overjoyed that I was still alive. My concussion subsided before I went into surgery, and even though I was high on sedatives, it was the only time through the entire ordeal when I felt like I was going to die: I was so dehydrated, and wasn't allowed any food or water whatsoever. I pitifully begged for just one sip of water. My dad took pity on my misery and whining and snuck me some illicit ice cubes. To this day I am extremely grateful for this.

I finally went into surgery and was put to sleep with anesthesia. The surgeons cut into my knee and inserted a metal rod. All of the places where the flesh had ripped were stitched back together: my ankle, inner calf, and knee.

Photo courtesy of Cherish Willis

Waking from an anesthetic sleep is sort of like being Rip Van Winkle. I had no idea where I was. I was really foggy because of the massive dosage of several drugs on top of the anesthesia. I remember a lot of people being there, so very happy I was still alive. I don't remember anything any of them said to me. I still had two legs, had dodged amputation. One of them was throbbing inside a splint, though.

My limbs were heavy, my mind cloudy and intoxicated. I was lying in a chair near my bed when I was told someone had come to see me. I wasn't able to think clearly or concentrate on anything, but then I noticed Rico, and I felt abruptly alive. I felt lighter and more flexible. I pushed myself up as he walked cautiously to my bedside. He told me he'd heard what had happened. He said he was sorry and he hoped I'd be OK. I was able to speak, but it was very incoherent. Nonsense, really. I took his hand and pulled him closer to me. He hesitated but gave in, probably feeling too sorry for the crippled blind girl in a hospital bed to decline. I threw my arms around him and collapsed into him both physically and emotionally. I began sobbing and begged for him to take me back, pleading in an intoxicated stupor to stay with me. His body was rigid and he didn't respond for a long time. He didn't say much of anything, and tried to back out gracefully, probably yearning to flee the room, but I'd have none of it.

Rico and I met two years before my car accident, my freshman year at Graves County High School. He spotted me at the beginning but I, being blind and oblivious, was almost completely unaware of his presence. He was a Mexican kid in my history class and the only student besides me who answered any questions. We were the smartest in the class by far. As it turns out, he'd spent months watching me from a distance—eating lunch by myself, sneaking off to the library to take naps—too anxious to actually approach me. He told me I had made a big impression on him with my antics: sitting on my desk at the beginning of class talking to Orpheus, laughing out loud, oblivious to spectators. After class one day he asked me to lunch, so we sat together talking about mutual interests and feelings. We both liked Japanese animation and other art, and we were both socially awkward and essentially friendless.

I finally had a legitimate friend, and we only grew closer with time, eventually beginning a relationship in January of my freshman year. He told me in the beginning that he just wanted to pick one girl and marry her. He didn't want to date or play games with several girls. I told him he was stupid and delusional and that isn't how life works, but he seemed steadfast in his intent. I knew he was a liar, or at the very least a delusional little boy, and I told him it would never happen: I was schizo and mentally unstable. I even introduced him to Orpheus, but he never minded.

I kept my guard up, remaining cynical, but happy. For about ten months, I worked hard to hide my true self from Rico, not to have a mental breakdown in front of him and scare him off. Then, one day in sophomore year, I had a meltdown in communications class. I made a complete fool of myself, screaming, sobbing, and rambling hysterically in the storage room while my other classmates listened from outside. After Rico coaxed me to calm down, I was sure he was going to leave me. It only seemed logical. But he said he wouldn't leave me over that. I was overjoyed, convinced that he really did love me. Ironically, that was probably the moment he first considered that I wasn't actually what he wanted.

Our relationship continued for another year. We became so close it was scary, but he was always very controlling of me, grabbing my arm, and literally refusing to let go when my friends would come up and ask to talk to me in private. He'd managed to scare all of them off, to alienate me and keep me completely for himself. When he later became distant, I tried desperately to figure out what had changed, but he wouldn't say. Our once-great communication had diminished to nothing. He no longer searched for me in the commons, we never had long philosophical conversations, he never kissed me before class, and I knew our relationship was crumbling. When we eventually cut it off, I was devastated. I began acting out in outrage and emotional instability and went to in-school detention for a week. I'd never attend my last day of detention that following week because I was in the hospital.

My sister said that when she came to see me after my surgery, I was knocked out cold. She gave up waiting for me to wake up, but when Rico came in it was like he flicked a switch. When I saw him in my hospital room, the memories of all that had transpired were stronger than the weight of my intoxication. I knew, even in my current condition, that he was all I had. He was the thing that brought me the most happiness, and our break up is what had brought about my decline. Without him, when I recovered and returned to school, I knew I'd be more miserable than I had ever been. I had to get him back, no matter what. I needed him to maintain my mental stability, and I didn't want to let him leave until this was accomplished. There was a lot of emotion but not a lot of coherence, and despite my delirious pleading and sobbing, I couldn't convince him to stay with me. Eventually, I reluctantly let him go and he bid me farewell. I was devastated. I'd failed to obtain what I'd lost, and he'd once again abandoned me. I think it was that incident on top of my slow sobering up that led to my deep hatred of him; I wanted vengeance, but I failed to make him miserable. Looking back now, I realize how foolish I was, that I did little more than anger and embarrass him.

Throughout my stay at the hospital and my rehabilitation, this feeling of subdued hatred would surface. *It's all his fault: my car accident, my anger, my sadness. He placed false hope in me, only to string me along for his own amusement and then cut me loose over the edge of a cliff.* I became increasingly hostile. I'd lash out at my family, or invisible people who looked like him. I realize and appreciate the love my family has shown me. It's instinctual for blood relatives to care for one another. But Rico hadn't known me my entire life, had no obligation to care for me. He'd *chosen me*, and that's all I'd ever wanted: for someone to choose to love me. But if someone can choose to love another person, they can also choose not to love another person; that's something people longing for affection always neglect to remember.

I spent a week and a half in the hospital at Vanderbilt. Every day, nurses would come in to check my blood pressure, my temperature, and ask if I needed medication. I was totally dependent on them and my mother to feed me because I was so medicated. I had to be helped to go to the restroom and even to take a shower. I had no sense of privacy, and though I appreciated the generosity, it was agitating to rely completely on others; I'd been doing that my entire life. When they gave me a walker, I felt like a little old lady and ran around about as well as one. My family told me to take it easy, to limp slowly and take breaks when needed, but I was restless.

When I was in public school, I was the strangest girl there. Not only did I talk to invisible people, dress head-to-toe in black, and use a giant weird camera and TV screen to see the board, but I also had smaller quirks: sometimes I'd abruptly break into a sprint down the hallway, run from class to class, swerving and dodging people like I was a car on a high-speed chase, coming to a dead stop, feeling energized as confused people stood around looking at me. After my accident, I would no longer run like that; I was restricted, further disabled, more incapable than ever before. Even before the accident, I'd always had a limp because of a stroke I had when I was an infant, but now it was even worse.

See, it's like this: I was born with a condition called hydrocephalus which traps fluid that travels from the head to the spinal cord, causing the skull to expand to compensate for increased volume. This can eventually lead to stroke, brain damage, and other problems. Around four months old, I spent a lot of time screaming and crying, so my parents eventually took me to the doctor to see what was going on. The doctor looked me over and said he didn't really know, but that I could just be given some sleep medication; if problems persisted, they could bring me back and run tests.

The next morning my grandmother went to check on me and found that after sleeping for several hours, I was awake, silent, and still. They took me back to the doctor and found that I'd had a stroke, causing blindness, hemi-paralysis on my left side, and most likely my mental defects. If my parents had demanded that the doctors run more tests instead of just going home the day before, all my physical and mental defects might have been avoided. This is the one thing that, despite my parents giving me a lot of love and a pretty good upbringing, I'll probably always resent them for.

It's hard for me to imagine what this whole ordeal must have been like for my parents. I know my mother feels a lot of guilt and regret over not being more aware of my condition, that she feels like she was selfish back then. I've asked my father how he felt about the whole thing, that his child was defective and would now probably be harder to care for. I said, "You probably didn't feel much, because you tend to be—I don't want to say emotionless...." He cut me off, laughing, and said that sometimes he was pretty emotionless. He said everything was just so overwhelming. It was just one thing after another, so he didn't really have time to let everything sink in. He said his mindset was sort of that you plan and prepare and do all you can, and that it's still not enough, so you've just got to roll with it and do the best you can given the circumstances. He's always been one of those people that sort of floats along, just going with the flow. I enjoyed this when I was younger because he is so easy going, but at the same time, he's so hard to read and figure out. He truly perplexes me.

After my stroke, they sent me to Kosair Children's Hospital in Louisville, and I spent about a month there with my parents. My dad says the days blurred together, sitting in that room, rows of beds separated only by curtains. As bad a shape as I was in, he says there were several children who had it much worse than I did. A nurse would come in and write names of newly arrived patients on the board and then erase names of patients who had passed away. He says it was really depressing watching them erase those names, and for the people he'd shared the room with to simply never come back, but that it was morbidly relieving because at least it wasn't me. I was still alive.

Throughout my Vanderbilt hospital stay, I was isolated and unstable, randomly becoming hysterical and incoherent. The staff declared that I wasn't mentally well and required me to attend a mental rehabilitation facility. When I got home from Vanderbilt, I was put on bed rest, told to lay down, not to get up, and that anyone in the house would be happy to help me if I needed anything. I felt like a princess: a blind, crippled, mentally unstable princess, laying up in bed with people waiting on me, high on Percocet and various other pain killers. But, after a week I was no longer allowed to lounge around, sullen and unproductive; it was time for me to move on and follow the doctor's orders to attend mental rehab for four months, every Monday through Friday, from 9:00 A.M. to 4:00 P.M., like a job, until the staff lost patience with me or felt I'd made sufficient progress to be thrown back into normal society.

The receptionist behind the little window at Four Rivers Partial Hospitalization Program was friendly, and, upon realizing I was a newcomer to the cesspool of mentally unstable teenagers, she escorted me to a small room with a few sofas and a TV up in the corner. I sat stiffly, nervously waiting for someone to walk me back to a hallway full of padded rooms where schizos discuss the faults of their actions with themselves. To my surprise, the other patients at Four Rivers weren't like that at all. I was somewhat disappointed. Here I was, sort of expecting to be the normal one, or at least in similar company. But no, even in rehab, where I figured *everyone* would be defective in some way, they still looked at me and whispered, "What's wrong with that girl? Why does she do that?" Even in rehab, I was the crazy one: epic fail.

Our days were very structured, with set times for everything, even restroom breaks. Every morning we'd arrive in the little room with the couches and wait for someone to come scan us with a metal detector, which seemed a bit over the top. I later found out that while they did confiscate lighters, paper clips, and knives, they weren't worried about people slitting their wrists in the bathroom as much as they were checking to make sure no one had a cell phone or anything that would disrupt the order of the establishment. After we were cleared with the metal detector, we proceeded to the dining area where the girls and boys sat at different tables. Apparently, even in rehab, people just can't keep it in their pants. A staff member would come around each morning and tell us which fast food joint we were getting lunch from and take our order. This was one of the best parts of the entire program, besides the hope of mental rehabilitation, of course.

We then walked into the main room where most of our daily rituals took place. One of those rituals was attending a course that the staff called "Social Skills." I remember hearing that term, "Social Skills," and thinking, "Yep, that is exactly what I need." It was a class to teach us how to interact with other people appropriately, how to survive and co-exist with other humans. I was the odd man out, the person people whispered about, and had become increasingly reliant on and fond of my friend Orpheus, the very reason I was alienated. As someone who is socially inept, some tips and strategies on how to feign normality, and a list of what to do and what not to do, seemed very helpful.

Photo by Cherish Willis

Every day, we were all required to walk up to a whiteboard with everyone's name and our current "level," or state of progress, and write a therapeutic goal for the day: "I will be positive," or, "I will have a great day," or whatever. "I will try not to kill anyone today" wasn't acceptable. After this we had two hours of silence when everyone did their schoolwork in order to keep our grades up while we were away. Then we all sat around in a circle and participated in something called Community, by far the most tedious part of the routine. One by one we stood up and said, *Hello, my name is so-and-so and I'm here for blah blah blah.* When I first arrived, almost everyone reported they'd come for their "anxiety and depression." I jumped on the bandwagon, not sure what else to say. Sure, I had anxiety and depression, but that wasn't the whole story as to why I was in rehab: I needed to figure out if I could get my shit together.

After introductions, we sat in a circle giving compliments to each other: *Hey I'd like to congratulate you for being slightly less idiotic than you were yesterday*. We voiced concerns: *I'm really worried that I might get arrested again*. We rated our days: *My day is like a negative 500 because my parents grounded me from my cell phone.* The day went on with other little classes on coping mechanisms, and lessons about why we shouldn't drop out of school or do drugs. In group therapy, we all wrote down two emotions we were feeling upon entering the room. One time, a kid wrote "Gleeful" and "Enraged" on his sticky note. I thought, *Uh, hello, need a dictionary, buddy?* I was no stranger to mixed feelings myself, though; I had a lot of different emotions about rehab. I had proclaimed to everyone on my first day that I was a misanthrope, then I had to explain that this meant I had a profound disdain for the human race. My psychiatrist challenged me to try to bridge the gap between myself and everyone else. I forced myself to learn to fake normality, and to socialize with others, something I'm still working on. I've never been good at interacting with people, and I broke down and sobbed once because I was afraid that I couldn't do it, couldn't coexist with others or function in society, the things everybody else seemed able to do. I had to prove myself wrong.

I forced myself into situations I would have otherwise strategically avoided and found some sort of joy interacting with the world. I even started to get excited for the end of the day when, for an hour, we got to socialize and kill time. I looked forward to playing cards, something you can't do on your own, and was actually happy to interact with these people. I realized that my problems were never going to go away, and unless I went into self-imposed seclusion, I was going to have interactions with people whether I wanted to or not. I might as well start practicing while I still had regular and immediate access to a therapist.

I was the only one who actually completed the program. On my last day, they threw a graduation party. The staff said I could have any treat I wanted to share with the class as a reward, so I chose one of those big cookie cakes. It had an owl on it and said "Congratulations!" The whole staff showed up, and they seemed genuinely happy for me. They all wished me well and said to come see them if I was ever in town. It meant a lot to me, being released and yet still welcomed back, because it meant they didn't just pass me through the program to get rid of me. I felt I had made progress and made a strong enough impression for them to want to see me again. It really was a warm feeling knowing that these people actually liked me.

Sometimes, I just wanted to quit and felt there was no point in being there. When I had conflicts with staff or my peers, I just wanted to shut down. At the end of the day, though, I excelled there. I learned a lot of valuable skills, and more importantly, I learned that I'm actually a likeable person. I still tend to consider myself a cynic and always try to be aware of human cruelty and selfishness, but I realized that despite this, I need to learn to coexist peacefully with others. I've also realized that I'm no better than anyone else. For the most part, we're all flawed, selfish, confused humans. Knowing this makes it much easier to empathize and get along with others.

After four months of rehab, I dreaded going back to school. I was certain I'd be completely alone and that there was nothing to gain from my old, underfunded, podunk school. There was nothing I could obtain there that I couldn't obtain somewhere else. Transferring to the Kentucky School for the Blind in Louisville seemed to be the answer to my predicament. I'd have a semi-new start, and if it panned out,

I felt it was very fitting for the mysterious transfer student to have a haunted room.

Photo by Cherish Willis

hopefully some insight as to how I should go about sustaining myself in the future. So my family and I decided that I would run away from my problems and all the negativity to potentially find something worthwhile. People come to KSB for many reasons, but my reason is not as romantic as some. Simply put, my motivation for moving four hours away from everything I knew was fear: fear of being alone, fear of having to explain to everyone what was wrong with me, fear of rumors I knew had surfaced at my public school that I'd been sent to an asylum for four months.

I was scared to go to KSB, too, because I'd attended short summer programs at KSB twice before, and I'd had some negative experiences: conflicts with peers and dorm parents, in part due to my own attitude and stupidity. But I'd made allies, too. I called one of them, a teacher named Bo Mullins, who had been my boss and instructor during the summer work program, and asked if he felt it'd be beneficial for me to come to KSB. He said yes and to think about it. I was nervous, cynical, and overall dismayed about moving to KSB full time.

When I arrived, I first had to be checked for lice, the flu, tuberculosis, plague, etc. After that, something horrifying happened: the nurse tried to take my drugs away. I clung to the prescription bottle and said they'd have to pry it from my cold, dead hands. They tried reasoning with me, saying that I wasn't allowed to self-administer the medication I needed for my anxiety, and that, furthermore, it was a safety precaution: that blind students might take meds that weren't theirs. I wasn't having any of it, but my mother ordered me to hand them over so she could drive back home to West Kentucky, four hours away. In a moment of frustration I said, "Fine. Have it." I pitched the bottle at the nurse's head, and stormed out of the room to my dorm. Later, I just got another bottle of pills and hid them in my underwear drawer.

My new room was at the end of the hall and was always very cold for some reason. People on campus said it was haunted. I felt it was very fitting for the mysterious transfer student to have a haunted room. Decorative paper signs with people's names hung on the doors to their rooms, ironically not written in braille. With three people in my room, I was sure I'd have no privacy. My roommates were Amanda, a developmentally disabled girl who always set her alarm for 5:30, to the aggravation of me and my other roommate, Len Remy. I didn't care for either of them initially. Len didn't speak English very well, but was really outspoken. I found her to be a bit much.

One time while my roommates were out, I turned the light off and took a nap only to be interrupted by the light turning back on. Len and some others in the dorm had walked in to hang out in the room. I lifted my head with slight agitation but decided to be civil. I asked them softly if they could please socialize somewhere else. Surprisingly, they complied and tried to get Len to leave the room too, but she wasn't happy about it. She huffed and stomped her foot and said in her thick Burmese accent, "No! It no sleep time! She need wake up!" After a few minutes of arguing and bargaining, she followed them out of the room and I went back to sleep.

Eventually Amanda moved out of the room, and it was just the two of us. Even with her limited English and limited knowledge of nap times, Len was the kind of blunt smart-ass I liked, and we became surprisingly close. Sometimes Len and I would just sit on her bed and talk smack. We had no filters and, as catty as it was, it was enjoyable. Sometimes, she'd come up to me and try to articulate that she'd like to borrow my straightening iron but only end up saying "You, you have...hair...hot..." while gently pulling her black hair between flat hands, trying to mimic the motion of the flat iron. I'd say, "You mean a straightener," and I'd make her repeat the word back to me in an effort to improve her English.

Along with academics, I learned something else that is crucial to my survival; feigning normality. I'll never be completely normal, but I'm at least a little better at keeping a lower profile. My grades improved, I was employed, my family ties were strong again, and I was able to cope with my car accident, essentially through morbid humor. The scars I used to hide didn't bother me as much now, and upon being asked about them, I informed people that I was "doing yoga in the road." I didn't have any more self-pity, nor did I have any negative feelings about my accident; I'd found a way to be open about my injuries and say exactly what I felt everyone was allowed to know without being awkward. I think I'd finally started to heal, and if I may be so self-flattering, had made a lot of progress.

Photo by Cherish Willis

One time Len, a bunch of other students, and I were in the practical living lab for some class. We got bored waiting for the food to cook so we started singing and twirling around the room doing the *stomp, stomp, clap* beat to "We Will Rock You." I was wearing a black, gothic, Lolita dress and pig-tails, singing Freddie Mercury's part, and before I realized it, everyone in the room had joined in. I looked around, and all of a sudden I didn't feel like the outlandish girl who couldn't sing or dance: I did so openly in front of people. I felt like I had finally found my place in that room and that I was surrounded by people who liked me. When we finished, we were all so hyped—screaming, carrying on, running around the room—that we had to be told to chill out. My blood was pumping and I left school that day feeling ecstatic. I was finally getting the hang of this "interacting with others" thingy.

That year I planned prom, won the meaningless title of prom queen, won awards for being on the forensics team, and graduated high school with three scholarships. Since then, I enrolled in college, made some friends, got an apartment, found a stable relationship, and, overall, I'm content. The irony is that in running away from my problems, they all sort of fixed themselves. I'm sure I'll have new problems now that I'm an "adult," but hopefully I'll be more mentally stable and able to handle them.

I've been in a relationship for two years with a guy named Jonathan McClure. We met through a mutual friend who he was trying to sleep with for a while. After many rejections, he set his sights on me and invited me to go on a four-wheeler ride in an attempt to woo and screw me. I was already in a relationship, albeit one that was crumbling and devoid of intimacy, and I didn't plan on giving this guy the time of day, but I still liked him and we had common interests. The date was really fun until he got the four-wheeler hopelessly stuck and we had to walk two miles back to his house through the heat and humidity of Wingo, Kentucky. He constantly had to take breaks and catch his breath because of his chronic bronchitis, and I kept tripping and stumbling as we made our way through the field of tall thicket and grass. Each time I tripped,

I looked around, and all of a sudden I didn't feel like the outlandish girl who couldn't sing or dance: I did so openly in front of people.

Photos courtesy of Cherish Willis

he caught me and asked if I was OK. Eventually he picked me up and carried me bridal style, but he started panting almost right away. It made me feel like I weighed 250 pounds.

Then he needed to rest, and there was a root protruding like an arch from the ground. He decided to sit there, only to have it snap in half and send him to the ground on his back. It was hysterical, definitely the funniest thing I'd seen in a long time. It was one of those moments you wish you had on record to send to *America's Funniest Home Videos*. I was bent over laughing so hard I couldn't breathe. He sighed in defeat, certain he would remain a virgin for another day. Eventually I regained my composure and stared down at him as he lay on the ground in defeat. I smiled at him and proceeded to lie down on his chest. As I looked into his surprised eyes, I began laughing again. He sighed and waited for me to finish. When I was silent, he wrapped his arms around me and was very soft-spoken—probably out of embarrassment—as he confessed that he liked me, that he'd arranged this day to try and impress me, and that he was very aware of his epic failure. I smiled at him and told him that I liked him too.

I stayed with him that night and after much chatting and cuddling, among other things, we began a relationship that, despite having its troubles as all relationships do, has brought me much happiness, stability and peace of mind. I still deal with the mental instability that I always have, but through medication and psychological assistance, I'm making it. I'm still alive, not homeless, not addicted to anything. I'm writing for an anthology of nonfiction. I'm not sure how far up I've come, but I'm no longer lying in the road bleeding to death, metaphorically or literally.

I recently bought my first home with the insurance money from the accident. Not long ago, I walked around the grounds of the condominium complex taking pictures and an old woman approached me and asked if I was a realtor, to which I replied that I was actually a tenant who already lived there. She smiled at me and informed me that I wasn't a tenant but a homeowner. I'm not sure why that impacted me so much, but it is true: that condo, that 1,070 square feet, is mine. Mine to paint, hang up pictures, and re-tile bathrooms as I please. That feeling is very liberating and empowering.

I have found that it brings me delight to make my living space look the way I want it to. There are more projects I'd like to do that will come with more time and money, but Jonathan and I are working on it little by little, getting a new comforter for the guest bedroom, putting pictures on the walls, and hanging curtains in my bedroom.

There are lots of places within walking distance if I need anything. It's relieving to feel more useful just being able to run little errands. I am still trying to figure out if I am cut out for work, whether I should finish school or get a job. I've contemplated doing nothing, just biding my time, but I'm too restless to be content with such a lifestyle. I'd like to find something, one thing, I can pride myself on besides surviving traumatic events. I've considered pursuing a career as a stunt double. I have a pretty good resume for it.

Photo by Cherish Willis

The choices we make daily

JAMIE BENJAMIN

My mom craves a life of fun and adventure, new places and new things, but she's a workaholic, so there's usually no time or energy for these activities. She always worked hard to make ends meet and provide for her kids. Still, when she came home, she'd have brought us each a candy bar, or rented a movie we wanted to watch so that we could spend time together as a family. It really is the little things. Her work ethic is truly admirable, and her thoughtfulness is touching. She's a kind person and she cares about our interests. I really appreciate that, and I hope that one day she'll be able to put herself first and work as hard at being happy as she's always worked to provide for us.

I was born in Paducah, Kentucky. My early childhood was fairly happy, until my parents divorced when I was nine or ten years old. When we were younger, my brother and I were very close and we played together all the time. After our parents divorced, we were very angry and confused and started to be hateful to each other. My dad had moved out and we didn't see him much, and my mom became hostile and vindictive. She suffered from a lot of mental health issues. She screamed and yelled and just did really mean things to us, like burn our toys.

Like, Honeycomb cereal had started putting posters of all the WWF wrestlers in the cereal boxes as prizes—you know, Hulk Hogan, the Ultimate Warrior, Andre the Giant, Macho Man Randy Savage—and it was a huge deal. We started eating all kinds of Honeycomb so we could get all of the posters. We put all the posters up on the wall, and we were very excited about them, and then one day we were arguing over whose posters belonged to who and our mom became mad, took all the posters down, and told us that we were going to divide them. We still couldn't get along and decide who ate all those boxes of Honeycomb to get this said poster. So our mom just ripped up all of the posters: six months of eating Honeycomb cereal, and she just ripped them up.

Mom remarried, but continued to do crazy things. Our stepfather had a really good job, so he went and bought a really good, brand new truck, and she threw paint all over it. She would get mad at him and shoot his truck with bullet holes. He had a tractor—tried to farm a little bit on the side—and she poured sugar in the tractor motor. She took her brand new Monte Carlo, which was a pretty fancy car back then, and decided to plow it over all of his tobacco that had just been planted. What's sad is that, when she's happy, she can really be a lively and entertaining person, but those moments where she is happy and entertaining are so few and far between that we rarely bother to reach out or see her.

High school was not a golden time for me. I was fifteen when I found out I was pregnant, and I was sixteen when you were born. I remember crying and being upset and thinking that my life was over. I completed my sophomore year, and went back my junior year, but I didn't stay very long. It was scary. Your dad and I were high school sweethearts. He was my first boyfriend, and I was young and stupid and thought that he hung the moon and that he was so cool. A note to teenage girls everywhere: cool isn't what makes a relationship successful. I was careless and just so eager to have someone to love me, because my mom never really showed us real love or affection.

Charlie swore up and down that he would love me and that he would take care of us and that everything would be fine. His family was really awesome and took us in. They were very poor. They had a run-down house, but they did take me in and they helped

She would get mad at him
and shoot his truck with
bullet holes.

Photo by Cherish Willis

Photos courtesy of Cherish Willis

take care of you, and then they helped us get a little place on their property and were very involved in our lives, and still are.

The house we shared with your dad's parents didn't have adequate heat or cooling. When you were four months old, you'd been sick and crying and crying and crying. I thought that the house was really hot, and that you were just miserable and irritable like the rest of us. I couldn't do anything to console you. Finally, my mother-in-law insisted that we go to the hospital, but they couldn't find anything wrong with you. They gave you a suppository to help you sleep, and said that the next morning you should be fine, but if there was anything else just go to a regular pediatrician.

You slept throughout the night, and then the next morning you were still asleep and I decided just to let you sleep and went downstairs to watch television and get some breakfast. My mother-in-law went to check on you and said that you were just still, your eyes were open but you couldn't move. So we all got dressed and went to the pediatrician, and the pediatrician immediately called an ambulance and rushed you to the hospital where we found out you'd had a stroke. I felt like it was my fault, that I should have been up first thing that morning checking on my daughter. I should have been there, been more concerned.

I still blame myself for that. If I had been a better mom, a more mature mom, that was in tune with my child, I would have insisted that all the necessary tests be run when we took you to the hospital the first time, and then you wouldn't have had a stroke. I was young and stupid and everything was about me, even though I loved my daughter. It was always, "Why is this happening to me? Why is my daughter sick?" It shouldn't have been about me, and I regret that to this day. I believe some of your mental health issues stemmed from the stroke. Looking back, sometimes I feel ashamed because I was so naïve and so blind to things. I realized that you would need more extensive professional help to get you in a good place; that's probably the only thing I realized at that point. If I'd have known what I know now, maybe you wouldn't have suffered through some of those things. I have a lot of regrets like that.

Ours was a very troubled marriage. Very distant. I had some mental health issues. I think I suffered from post-partum depression. He didn't help take care of the children. Our relationship became hostile. He chose to spend more and more time away with his friends. He got a video camera, and they would go around filming themselves skateboarding or making fools of themselves at Walmart. I was at the house alone, taking care of a sick child, pregnant again with your sister Tatum. There was no money, so I'd get jobs waiting tables or stripping tobacco, and I'd have to pay someone to watch you so I could work. So it just crumbled. He eventually left with a coworker, and I was left with my children and ended up moving out from the home where we lived together. I found an apartment, and started school. I got my GED and then attended college. I needed to get some kind of education in order to take care of my children. I didn't have a plan of what I wanted to study, I just wanted to start school and see if anything caught my interest. I became interested in psychology, and that is what my degree is in. My minor was in behavioral studies.

Several years after the divorce, I married a gentleman in the military, Adam. We moved to El Paso and had a son together. I was very far away from my family, who I'd never really been away from. We struggled financially. Eventually, I did gain employment at a gas station on base. I had several friends and coworkers who became like family to me, which was the one bright spot of being in El Paso. I still communicate with some of them on Facebook.

I really did not like El Paso. Our marriage was fairly violent. Adam drank a lot, and since he drank a lot I did too, and we would get in very explosive arguments. The police came to our house a few times because of our arguments. He was a lot younger than I was, so he just wasn't ready for marriage. Our marriage lasted approximately three years. We decided that the marriage wasn't going to work, and then me and my children moved back home to Kentucky.

I speak with Adam once every two or three months, and we get along fairly well for the sake of our son. Even though he's not here to help physically, he does help financially. He also doesn't interfere in how I see fit to raise the child.

When we moved back to Kentucky, we moved into our Aunt Frances' house in Benton, Kentucky. The only reason I agreed to live there was because I thought it was going to be rent free, which it was for the first month. They were going to let me live in it to keep it in good shape and keep it clean while Aunt Frances was in the nursing home, but she died soon after, and then the estate made us start paying rent.

Aunt Frances' house was really old and had this really creepy basement that looked like it had torture objects hanging down from the ceiling. I was scared to go downstairs. The water heater would continuously go out, so I would have to go downstairs all the time and make you kids hold the flashlight so I could get down on my stomach and light the heater. I eventually taught you kids how to do the laundry so I wouldn't have to go downstairs to do it anymore; your imaginations didn't run as wild as mine did.

When you started talking to people that nobody else could see, sometimes it scared me, because I've always believed in spirits and demons. You would say things like, "There's somebody in my closet," and I'd be like, "Don't tell me things like that! I don't want to know things like that." I felt sorry for you a lot of times, because I believed it was more being lonely and feeling like you didn't fit in with all the kids at school, so you wanted to have imaginary friends. As you got older and violent episodes progressed, we figured out that it was a mild form of schizophrenia. It's just part of who you are. I love every part of you. You're an eccentric little soul.

High school was very, very hard for you. I think in some ways you made it harder on yourself by wearing your cosplay costumes, because it drew attention to you from the other students. They would make fun of you, and then in turn you would make a scene or become very upset about it. I think high school is hard for any teenage girl, but it was about ten times harder for you. I wanted to encourage any friendships that I possibly could. You made friends who I might not have necessarily picked out for you, but just the fact that you had people you felt you could relate to meant a lot to me. I wanted to be supportive of those.

When you had your car accident, that was really scary. You got taken by helicopter to Vanderbilt. That night, I was completely in shock, and just sort of numb. I stayed in the hospital with you and I don't think I cried. It was just very, very hard. I was in mom mode. I didn't have time to feel.

Because you were so hysterical, they put a watch on you, and they had this Brunhilde-looking woman—two long, blonde braids, looked like she'd come out of the Marines. I was trying to help you to the restroom, and I was like, "Now just pull the door shut a little bit," because I didn't want her to see you using the bathroom, and she yelled at us, "Oh no. Oh no. She's not going to shut that door. That door will stay open while I'm in here." I got angry with her, and I'm like, "I'm the mom, and you're not in charge here. I'm in charge here." So we got into this argument, and I said something to her that was really hateful, and I went and got the nurse, and then she and the nurse got into it. You were just sitting there laughing your little butt off like a hyena, and I'm like, "It's not funny. Quit laughing."

It was hard when I sent you to the boarding school. I know that you thought I was just trying to get rid of you, but I really was sending you there to gain some independence. I did not like you being gone at all, and then you stayed up there for your senior year, and then you didn't move back. So it's like you haven't really been home for two years now.

Really, my only disappointments are that I still don't have a fulfilling career, that my marriages didn't work out, and that I still haven't found the right person. I like the person I've become, for the most part. I'm definitely more responsible than I was when I was younger. I'm a better person all the way around. I'm smarter. I make better choices. There are a lot of enjoyable parts of my life. I like to explore different ideas of spirituality. I'm interested in religion. I like some of the new age things, such as crystals and essential oils and natural healing and natural foods as healing agents. I've taken jujitsu before, I've taken tae kwon do, I'm currently taking guitar lessons, yoga lessons. I like exploring something new: going to a new beach and taking surfing lessons, or going to a new mountain and hiking to a new waterfall with my kids and my best friend and my sister and my brother.

I have lots of really good friends, I have my church family, and I have two beautiful daughters and a precious son. I think you are making really good choices and doing really well. Your sister is working and learning the value of her work, and your brother is sweet and kind and loving, and hopefully he stays that way.

There was no family unity when I was a child, but Dad was a great source of strength and pride. The older I get, the more I want to be like him. He is the kindest and hardest working man I've ever known, the most giving man, also the most rigid. He has very firm beliefs on how people should act, and I respect that, even though I don't agree with some of those beliefs. He taught me hard work, to be a respectful person, to be a godly person, to be a strong person. I try to live up to his examples and work hard and treat others fairly, and be a good person and a good Christian.

I don't know if I'm more patient than my mom, but I try to empathize with my children and help them make decisions, not just tell you what to do. I listen to you, I discuss things with you, I encourage you to have your own opinions, I don't belittle your opinions. Even though on occasion I do lose my temper, I don't scream and yell on a daily basis or try to lower your self-esteem. I try to be an encouraging mother and I try to be an active part of your lives.

I spent a lot of years making wrong choices and also hating myself for those choices. People grow up when they're ready to grow up. Sometimes they're forced to grow up. But once you can get to a place where you can prioritize, nothing is more important than family. If I want to leave anything with my kids, some ideas or concepts, it's that your past will always shape who you become, but that we are also products of the choices we make daily. So even though I made horrible choices in my past, the things that I've done the last few years have gotten me on the right path.

Photo by Jessica Ebelhar

ACKNOWLEDGMENTS

Like all Louisville Story Program endeavors, this book seeks to amplify the voices of individuals who are members of a larger community. And, like all LSP endeavors, the larger community has supported the effort. We are grateful to these individuals and organizations for their encouragement and assistance in producing this book.

To the faculty and staff of the Kentucky School for the Blind, especially Kyrstin Price, Elaine Hall, Terry Burger, and Ben Wright, for their wise counsel and dedication to our project.

To the families of the authors who have shared their own stories, donated their time, and championed the book: Brandy and Chris Atherton, Debby Hancock, Lloyd and April Caudill, Ken and Angelita Tirey, Alisa Hall, Sue Carmen, Mike and Jennifer Lowe, Aubrey Compton, Anna Nichole Waller, Lisa Mathers, and Jamie Benjamin.

To the major funders of this project: the Snowy Owl Foundation, the Kentucky Arts Council, the Arthur K. Smith Family Foundation, the Kentucky School for the Blind Charitable Foundation, Brown-Forman, the CHAMP Foundation, the Gilbert Foundation, and the Louisville Downtown Lions Club.

To Shellee Marie Jones, for honoring our authors' voices and narratives with incredibly graceful design throughout the book. As always, it has been a joy to work with you.

To all of wonderful folks at the American Printing House for the Blind, for believing in this project from the very beginning, for producing and distributing braille and large print editions of the book, and for many good ideas.

To Savannah Barrett for her encouragement, patience, thoughtful perspective, and expert assistance.

To our foundationally important friends at Kertis Creative for their continued generosity, incisive understanding of LSP's goals, and beautiful photography and videography.

To Jessica Ebelhar, whose remarkable photos are found in every chapter of this book, for donating her time and prodigious talent.

To Letitia Quesenberry, a brilliant artist with a huge heart, for creating the stunning cover art.

To Spalding University, for their partnership. We're honored to call your campus our home.

To Metro Councilman Bill Hollander, for his enthusiasm and support for the project.

To the Kentucky Talking Book Library, for volunteering to translate this book into audio format.

To all local bookstores and other businesses who sell our books.

To all of the generous supporters of the Kickstarter campaign and other donors, especially: Gerald Abner, Cayo Alba and Michael Frick, Tyler and Chenoweth Allen, the American Printing House for the Blind M.C. Migel Library, Jessica Belcher, Emily Bingham and Stephen Reily, Cassiopia Blausey, Doug and Sandy Compton,

Tom Cottingham, Roy and Julie Elis, Claudia Gentile, the Kentucky Council of the Blind, the Kentucky School for the Blind Alumni Association, Judy Look and Fred Look, DMD, Kristen Lucas, Bob and Bo Manning, Elizabeth Matera, Laurianne Matheson, Beth and Doug Peabody, Damaris Phillips and Darrick Wood, Kyrstin Price, Kevin Sachs, Holly Sadow, Joan Shelley, David Tachau, Kent Thompson and Cassie Stokes, Phil and Landis Thompson, and Lynn Winter.

Our deepest thanks to the many other people who have supported and encouraged the authors, this project, and/or the Louisville Story Program. And thank you, reader, for listening to what the authors have to say.

Joe Manning and Darcy Thompson
Louisville Story Program

Photo by Jessica Ebelhar